T0064089

Little Barbara

In a family of fourteen: Mother, Father, Twelve Children. Nine girls and three boys.

GAIL ALCINA

authorHOUSE®

AuthorHouse™ LLC
1663 Liberty Drive
Bloomington, IN 47403
www.authorhouse.com
Phone: 1-800-839-8640

© 2014 Gail Alcina. All rights reserved.

No part of this book may be reproduced, stored in a retrieval system, or transmitted by any means without the written permission of the author.

Published by AuthorHouse   09/19/2014

ISBN: 978-1-4969-0259-7 (sc)
ISBN: 978-1-4969-0258-0 (e)

Library of Congress Control Number: 2014906222

Any people depicted in stock imagery provided by Thinkstock are models, and such images are being used for illustrative purposes only.
Certain stock imagery © Thinkstock.

This book is printed on acid-free paper.

Because of the dynamic nature of the Internet, any web addresses or links contained in this book may have changed since publication and may no longer be valid. The views expressed in this work are solely those of the author and do not necessarily reflect the views of the publisher, and the publisher hereby disclaims any responsibility for them.

CONTENTS

INTRODUCTION

Our journey starts on my birthday in May 1942 on a sharecropping farm in Albany, Georgia. For those who are unfamiliar with sharecropping, that is a great place to start. This plan has been around since ancient Egypt and it especially became essential after the Civil War ended in 1865. When the slaves were set free, they needed to work and earn a living. Many of them bought into this concept and worked the land for the rich folk. It was a step up from slavery because the land owners were not permitted to abuse or whip them.

Whole families were expected to take care of the planting of new crops, tending and harvesting. In exchange for their back-breaking work, they were given a place to stay (usually a poorly built shack) and a portion of the crops that translated into a small amount of money.

Many land owners ran a store on their own land and jacked up the prices so the workers could not afford to buy necessities. Often they went into debt and had to continue working to pay off their debts. The cycle continued for many generations until they became debt free—if ever.

Multiple generations were raised in this fashion.

By 1942 when I entered the scene, things had improved greatly. As part of a sharecropping agreement my father made, he was the one expected to raise and take care of the produce. We were not slaves but sometimes my father must have felt that way.

More than anything else you might find in this book, the main message is to let you know the value of family. There's not a single family on this planet that doesn't have problems every now and then. Working through them is what makes us strong.

Farm life wasn't easy and of course all was not perfect for this family of sharecroppers. We loved each other and that is what kept us going. Love tied us together through the struggles, pains, insecurities, and deceptions and made our joyous moments even more memorable.

I ask that you take this journey with me where you'll meet many of my family members, friends, neighbors, and learn that no matter what you come against, *FAMILY* is most important.

Family Members

Father	Gilbert Lee McKay
Mother	Barbara Ann McKay

Siblings

Antoinette Ruth McKay

Hope Hana McKay

David Dean McKay

Hilary Rita McKay

Della Rose McKay

Mabel Maria McKay

Lucille Fran McKay

Tyler Glen McKay

Sherry Fay McKay

Barbara Ann McKay

Romeo Devin McKay

Golda Carla Mckay

CHAPTER 1

Birth of Barbara

The day I came into this old world wasn't a good day for my mother. She was in labor for a long time and her pains were almost unbearable. The other births of her children were nothing like this. The midwife and grandma were trying to help however this time they needed help and dad had to get the doctor. Mom knew something was really wrong when the doctor arrived at the house. He examined mom and told her that this was a big headed baby this time. He said "I have to get something to help you with pushing because you can't do it by yourself. The doctor told my daddy to go to the store and get a small bottle of castor oil, warm it up and give it all to her to drink. In about an hour here I came castor oil and all (smile). I was born on a farm share cropping for Mr. Whitehead in Albany Georgia. Share cropping was what my mother and father did with my older sisters and brothers.

Mom said I was a beautiful and smart child. I was walking and talking and could call all my siblings by their first names and was the easiest one to potty train before I was one year old.

I was born May 12, 1942 with pretty black curly hair and beautiful brown skin. My sister Hope was married and pregnant and loved combing my hair. Hope liked combing my hair and someone told her if she combed my hair while she was pregnant that her child would have curly hair too. I don't know if that was why her child was born with curly black hair. It was much curlier than mine. To this day he still has his curly hair. However, today with all the perms and hot combs I've had in my hair all my curly hair is gone now.

Some of the first things I remember after my birth were my dad coming home drunk and raising all kinds of hell. I remember my siblings picking on me about my big head the first day of school. We had to walk to and from school. I was too little to walk that far so Tyler would put me on his back and carry me home. This was when I realized I was very mean. I didn't want anyone to touch me only my family.

I remember one day I woke up and my oldest brother David was gone. My sister Hilary got married and she and her husband Leon had a little boy, Parker. They were also share cropping for Mr. Whitehead and at that time I was too small to pick cotton. I was only five or six years old and Hilary asked mom if I could babysit for her. The cotton field was next to the house. Mom said yes if it's ok with Barbara. I felt like a big girl. I said yes and everything went alright for a while, then one day I tasted the baby's milk and it was good. I put the bottle in his mouth for a little while and then I put it in my mouth longer. He started crying and crying, (Parker). At that moment I was in another world sucking on his bottle.

Hilary heard her baby crying and she came home to see what was wrong. That's when she caught me sucking her baby's bottle. I got mad because she caught me and said I will never babysit for her again. She said I am not mad with you, just don't do that again. I knew she was mad but she didn't have anyone else to keep her baby. I told her I will keep her baby and I would not suck his bottle again. I didn't suck the baby's bottle again. Hilary fed her baby and went back into the field.

Later her husband went to town to sell the cotton. Hilary asked me to help her catch a chicken for their supper. I helped her and she tied the chicken to the fence to cut the chicken's head off. Hilary got the knife and couldn't cut the head. She looked like she was going to cry. I told her to give me the knife and I cut the chicken's head off. Blood was all over both of us from her picking me up so I could reach the chicken. It looked like someone had cut us up. I helped Hilary pick feathers off the chicken and Hilary did the rest by herself. Then I told her I wanted to go home. We only lived a little ways down the road. Hilary went in the road and called mom to tell her I was coming home. When I started down the road she said I will save you a piece of chicken for helping me. I said thank you as mom stood by the side of the road waiting for me to come home. When I got to her she asked what happened to you, she thought I had gotten cut.

I told mom I was alright, that I cut the chickens head off for Hilary that's all. Mom picked me up and said you did all that? I said yes. Then I said Hilary is chicken and a scary cat. Mom and I had a big laugh, then said let me take those bloody clothes off before your dad gets home and has a heart attack when he sees you like this.

Dad came home and I told him what I did to help Hilary. He told me I was a big girl; keep up the good work helping others like your big sister.

Mom told dad her chicken order was at the store. They went to get the little chicks. Dad had finished the chicken coop days ago. Everything was ready. This time she ordered about one hundred chickens. She had about ten Roosters. She would sell some of the chickens and the eggs and keep some for the house. She gave some of the chickens to her sister's, brother's' mother and father and the rest of the family.

CHAPTER 2

The Little Blue Dress

One afternoon after mom and dad had finished placing all the chickens in the coop, dad was working outside in the yard while mom was inside cleaning out her trunk. I was trying to help when I saw a pretty, blue dress in the trunk. I asked mom, "Can I have the dress?" But before she could answer me, dad called for her to come outside. She went to see what he wanted.

With curiosity, I picked up the pretty, blue dress and put it next to me. It was my size and I just knew mom was going to give me this dress. I put the dress neatly back inside the trunk and waited and waited for mom to come back. It was a very long time to wait and before she could come back, I decided to try on the little blue dress. Just at that moment mom walked into the room. She slapped the piss out of me; I mean the real thing. It was running down my legs. Mom grabbed the dress and almost pulled my head off as she yanked it over my head. Getting the dress off I ran into my dad's arms. I was crying my heart out.

I had never been hit that hard before. Dad held me for a little while until I stopped crying so loud. When he put me down, I grabbed and held onto his legs with all my might. I was holding on for dear life. Dad asked me what was wrong and I told him mom had slapped me for nothing. He said, "Your mom didn't slap you for nothing so what did you do?"

I said, "Yes she did. I just tried on the blue dress in the trunk."

By that time mom was calling me. I grabbed onto dads' legs again and he picked me up and said, "Don't be afraid of your mother."

I pleaded with him, please don't let her get me." At that time he saw mom's hand print on my face. I was begging and begging dad not to let mom get me. My face still burned and pained me. I didn't want or need another slap.

Mom called me again and Dad said to Mom, "Barbara, let me talk to her." He put me on his knees and began to tell me that the little blue dress that I tried on was my sister's.

I asked, "Where is she and why didn't she wear her dress?"

Dad said with a hint of sadness in his voice, "Her name was Della Rose McKay and she died when she was about three years of age. The little blue dress is the only thing your mother has to remember her by."

At that moment I felt sorry for Mom and Dad. I was still mad with mom about what she had done to me. She could have told me about Della and told me not to touch the dress. Instead she slapped the hell and piss out of me. I didn't want Mom anywhere near me. I stayed outside with Dad all day.

When I saw Mom coming toward me I ran and grabbed Dad's legs. My two sisters, Mabel and Lucille, cooked supper. They called Dad and me in to eat. I asked Dad to let me sit next to him. He agreed. I really don't think he liked what Mom did to my face but he didn't make me go to her. He kept me near him. When we got to the table, Mom called me to come to her. I looked at Dad. Then she said, "I only want to put some medicine on your face." I still didn't move. Dad said, "I will put it on little Barbara; she'll be alright tomorrow."

Mom didn't say a word about putting the medicine on me until she saw her hand print on my face. I wasn't going to let her touch me because I didn't know if she was going to slap or hurt me some more. I stayed close to Dad everywhere he went. I was with him until Mabel and Lucille took me and two other siblings to get washed up and ready for bed.

The next morning Dad went to town to do some shopping. I was still in bed asleep when Mom walked into the bedroom. When I heard her voice I immediately jumped up. Mom said to me, "I am not here to hurt you; I only want to talk to you. I am sorry I slapped you," she said. "I was shocked when I saw you in Della's dress. In that blue dress you looked like Della. When I realized it wasn't Della, I just lost it." When she heard me crying and crying that brought her back to her senses. Mom said "Please forgive me. I am sorry. I am so sorry." She hugged and kissed me over and over. Then we were alright again. I knew my Mom loved me and I loved her too.

CHAPTER 3

Burned Left Hand

After the disaster with the little blue dress, there were many more situations. Mom and Dad didn't like me eating with my left hand. They felt this made me different from the rest of the children. I was the one they had to call the doctor for to deliver me, now I'm the only one left handed. I felt like the odd ball of the family. They had to change me to be the same as the rest of my siblings.

At first they didn't try to change me because at times I tried to eat with my right hand but the older I got, I used my left hand more. Mom and Dad really wanted me to use my right hand only. I put my spoon in my right hand but switched it back to my left hand. This continued over and over until one day my dad took a piece of string and tied my left hand behind my back.

This went on and on and I still tried to eat with my right hand, however the food would drop on me, onto the plate or on the floor. Not much food went into my mouth; Dad being upset said, "If you don't learn to eat with your right hand then you won't eat at all." I had to sit and try to eat with the right hand while my siblings ate. I cried and cried, finally after everyone had finished I ate alright.

Mom untied my hand when no one else was around and gave me something to eat. I felt like I was in jail. For some reason dad listened to my mom's dad more than his. Mom said dad was more like his own dad in his ways. Grandpa would stop by to visit every now and then. When he came on a visit he was very angry with mom and dad to see my hand tied behind my back. Grandpa sternly told them, "Untie that gal's hand. If God wants her to be left handed then so be it." That was the end of my hand being tied behind my back. Dad untied my hand and I ran to my grandpa who picked me up and I gave him a big hug. He gave me a kiss and I was so very happy.

I didn't have to go through having my hand tied behind my back ever again.

As soon as I got over one thing, here came another. All of my life, as far as I can remember, I would go to sleep early. Every day about five o'clock and sometimes before five when supper time came, someone in the family had to wake me up to eat.

Mom and Dad had to go into town one day and left my two older sisters in charge of us. They asked if they could cook fried chicken and grits and Mom told them, 'yes'. After catching the chickens cleaning and cooking them Mable called us to eat. Everyone went to the dining room except me. I was asleep in the living room.

Mabel came and woke me up and I went into the dining room, sat down and went back to sleep with my hand in the plate. Lucille had the hot grits pot and was putting grits in each plate when Mable called and asked, "Where should I put Mom and Dad's food?

She responded, "On top of the stove, in the warmer." Before she could turn back to see what she was doing, Lucille put a big spoon of hot grits on my hand. I woke up screaming and hollering and shaking my hand. My skin was flying all over the dining room. My sisters were more upset than me. They didn't know what to do. My hand was bleeding and all the skin on the back of my hand was gone. Mable put some cold water on my hand which helped a little. I know they thought Mom and Dad were going to beat the cowboy shit out of them.

Mom and dad came back at the right time. Mom got some spider web and put it on my hand to stop the bleeding. I thought Lucille was going to get a whipping. Mom calmly said, "It was just an accident."

In my mind I said to myself, I try on a little blue dress and mom almost slapped my head off leaving all five of her fingers imprinted on my face. When Lucille burned my hand they made me feel like it was my fault. I was asleep and Lucille should have looked to see what she was doing. I know she didn't do it on purpose, but she was older than me and should have known better. My hand got all burned up from carelessness and it was an accident.

My hand wasn't getting any better so Mom and Dad took me to Grandpa Edgar's house. He put some medicine on it which made it feel a lot better, a whole lot better. He made an ointment from rattlesnake and other things to be rubbed on my hand. Grandpa was a healer and a reader. He took care of my hand until it was all healed. To this day I still have the scar on my left hand.

While it was healing I couldn't use either one of my hands. My Grandma had to feed me until I could feed myself. I stayed with them until I was better and I went back to the farm with mom, dad and my siblings.

I was glad to be home. Mr. Whitehead stopped by one day and asked me what happened to my hand. I told him what happened. He told me, "Tell your sister to be more careful and watch what she's doing at all times." I told her what Mr. Whitehead said, she told me to tell Mr. Whitehead to go to hell because he couldn't tell her what to do.

CHAPTER 4

Mom and the Other Woman

My dad was a hard-working man. Beside working and drinking he had other women. Most men have one woman on the side, my dad had two. Mom knew Dad had women on the side and didn't care as long as he didn't bring them in her face. She didn't say a word until dad got his new truck and his woman, Mrs. Ginny, started disrespecting her.

When Mrs. Ginny would see Dad's new truck she would come running up to the truck, not caring who was in the truck with him. She would run to the truck and start talking to him in front of Mom and me. One day Mom said, "Ginny stay the hell away from my husband, if I catch you talking to him again, I will beat your ass. Do you hear me? You are going to respect me. I'm not going to tell you again. I am for real, you do it again I will show you better than I can tell you, just wait and see."

I don't know what my Dad had, but I know Mrs. Ginny was crazy about him. Everyone was telling her to stay away from him when he was with his family. Mrs. Ginny didn't listen to anyone. One Friday we were coming from Mom's parents' Mrs. Nester Lue Fulbright and Mr. Edgar Fulbright and her sister my Aunt Denise house. They all lived together. We went over there to help them kill four hogs.

On our way home, Mom asked Dad to stop by Shamrock, where mom worked on the weekends. Mrs. Mavis, the owner, would close for about two to three hours to show cowboy movies. She closed the bar because young, underage children came to see the movies. After the movies were over and the young people were gone, she would open back up.

When Dad stopped and Mom got out, I asked if I could go along. She helped me out of the truck and we went inside. Dad stayed in the truck and guess who was there? Mrs. Ginny! She was sitting at the bar with *two* men. Mom went to talk with Mrs. Mavis about how much fish they needed. Mrs. Mavis asked to borrow a big pan from mom. She forgot and left it in the truck. Mom said to me, "Little Barbara, stay here with Mrs. Mavis until I get back."

On her way to the truck, she noticed Mrs. Ginny wasn't at the bar anymore; it was only the two men. Mom walked outside, there was Mrs. Ginny talking to Dad. She looked up and saw Mom and tried to ease her ass past Mom.

Mom said, "Oh hell no, bitch, your ass is mine. I told you to stay the hell away from my husband." Mom grabbed her and spun her around. She slapped the piss out of her and started beating Mrs. Ginny all over her head. She grabbed a Pepsi Cola bottle off the counter and continued beating her with the bottle all over her body over and over again. Mom kicked Mrs. Ginny's legs from under her. Mrs. Ginny fell and when she tried to get up mom got on her back and kept beating her with that bottle.

Mom continued yelling, "When I get finished with you, you won't be able to sit on your ass. You will not want another married man." Mom hit Mrs. Ginny one more time in the head. She knocked her out for a few minutes. Then mom went to talk to Mrs. Mavis. Mrs. Ginny was all bloody when she regained consciousness.

One of the men at the bar, Mr. Don, said, "I told you one day Mrs. Barbara was going to beat your ass for messing with her husband."

No one tried to stop the fight, not even Mrs. Mavis or the other two men. Mr. Drew laughed at Mrs. Ginny getting up off the floor. He said, "Mrs. Barbara beat the hell out of you. Maybe you will think twice before you mess with Gilbert Lee McKay again."

Someone told Dad about what was happening inside. He came in and got me and put me in the truck. I told dad to wait for mom but he took off without her. I started yelling, "Go back and get mom!" But he kept right on going. I started to cry.

Dad said, "Don't cry! Everything will be alright." I kept crying and crying as I begged him to go back and get mom. No such luck.

He kept on going and telling me everything would be alright. When we got home Dad got out and helped me out. Then he went walking toward the barn. My siblings asked, "Where is Mom? He didn't open his mouth.

They asked me and I told them she was at the Shamrock fighting Mrs. Ginny. I guess Dad was mad because Mom beat the hell out of his woman's ass. Tyler got his rifle. Mable got the gun, Lucille got the axe, Sherry got the baseball bat and down the road they went to finish off Mrs. Ginny. They got half way there and met Mom coming home. Mom stopped them saying, "Ya'll don't have to do nothing to Mrs. Ginny. I took care of her. Every time she sees Gilbert, she will think about the ass whoopin' I gave her."

My siblings still wanted to beat Mrs. Ginny's ass for messing with our dad. At that time we didn't think Dad was messing with her so we put all of the blame on Mrs. Ginny. Mom said, "It was not a fight; I just beat the bitch's ass, that's all."

After what mom did to Mrs. Ginny, Dad told all his women when they saw him with his family to stay away and not to say a word to him. He said, "That's my wife, I demand respect for her and my children. She comes first no matter what." After knowing what mom had done to Mrs. Ginny everyone knew from then on to respect the family. The other woman Mrs. Gladys had always given Mom respect and never tried to disrespect the family. She didn't run around with Dad, he would go to her. Mrs. Gladys was an older, wiser woman. We knew about all of this because Dad would tell us when he was drunk; he was like a magpie when he drank.

About three months later Mrs. Ginny saw Dad's truck. Mom, Dad and I were in the truck. Mom and I got out and went into the store. She couldn't wait for us to go in the store. Here came Mrs. Ginny running to the truck to talk to Dad. He asked her, "Why's your head so damn hard? I told you to stay the hell away from me when I'm with my family."

She said, "It's alright, they went into the store."

Dad yelled at her, "You damn fool! I make the rules not you. Now get the hell away from me!"

Mrs. Ginny didn't move, Dad knocked her in her mouth and then she walked away. That's when Mom and I came out the store and saw Mrs. Ginny holding her mouth and walking away. Dad took us home and went back to town. She had a big, fat lip. Her son, Mr. Luke, tried to jump Dad to beat him up, but Dad turned it the other way around. After that Mrs. Ginny started giving mom respect. There was no more disrespect. No, none at all! Mrs. Ginny stopped running up to Dad's truck.

CHAPTER 5

Mom's Garden

Upon getting the respect she deserved from Mrs. Ginny, Mom turned her attention to her garden. Dad always got Mom's garden ready during planting season for her to plant seeds. He didn't use fertilizers in her garden because her garden was all organic. He put mule manure in her garden to make the vegetables grow beautifully. Mom had one small garden next to the house and two acre's next to the cotton field. No one in our little town planted many vegetables unless they were taking them to market to sell.

Mom sold her vegetables, too, but not in the market. She would sell to people in our little town. However, she gave away lots of them to family and friends and did a lot of canning the rest for winter. Some of the vegetables she planted were string beans, lima beans, pinto beans, okra, corn, tomatoes, sweet peas, watermelon, sweet potatoes, white potatoes, yellow turnips, cabbage, collard greens, mustard greens, peppers, onions, and a whole lot more. I think Mom was thinking about all the poor people in our town. She knew we were poor and that's why helping others less fortunate gave her a sense of joy.

The people who were unable to plant or go to the market for vegetables were her mission of blessing. Those most in need were the elderly, children, and those sick and feeble. She started taking me with her when she went to deliver the produce. I didn't mind too much because it kept me from getting into fights at home.

My siblings picked on me about my big head. I was tired of it and started beating them up. Sometimes I got two whippings in one day for fighting. Remember me telling you all that I was mean? Oh yes, I was something else! I was like a little tiger.

My brother said, "Your body weight was two pounds and your head weight was eight pounds," and then the fight was on. I looked like my Mom but I had a temper like my Dad. This was the reason she took me with her—it stopped me from getting so many whippings.

We were on our way to take an old lady, Mrs. Newlin, some food. Before we got there the wagon got stuck in the mud. Nell the mule couldn't pull us out. Mom gave me the rope, I was so scared, but she said, "Don't be afraid, everything will be alright". She put on her boots and got out the wagon and said, "When I tell you to, you pop Nell on her backside and say as loud as you can, '*Get up Nell! Pull, pull, pull!*' Say it over and over." Nell was pulling and Mom was pushing.

Mom and Nell got us out of the mud and we finally reached Mrs. Newlins house with the food. Mrs. Newlin was thankful for the food and happy to see us. Mom said, "We are going back the long way that will make me happy." We stayed for a spell and then returned home. Mom took food to her father, Mr. Edgar Fulbright; his wife, Mrs. Nester Lue Fulbright; her sister Denise; Dad's father, Mr. Garrett McKay and his wife, Mrs. Linetter Bell McKay; sister Laura Rose McKay Benedick and others. Mom gave food to black and white, to anyone who needed food. She even planted rice which came up once but the place where the rice was planted wasn't wet enough to produce rice.

Everyone in our little rural area knew Mom, me, her one-horse wagon and Nell, the mule.

It is now the end of vegetable season. Early that morning we went to take some food to Mrs. Bell. She was the last one to receive from the vegetable harvest.

When we returned home Mom said to me go gather the eggs. Most of the time while gathering eggs, I would start inside the chicken coop but for some reason this time, I started outside. When I got to the door of the coop I had the shock of my little life, scared out of my wits I saw a big chicken snake in the coop. It had a hen in its mouth. I didn't know a snake could open its mouth that wide. That chicken was going down his throat. I was so scared I couldn't move. I tried yelled for my Mom but she didn't hear me.

She said, "I had a feeling something was wrong with you." She came running, when she got to me and saw the snake, she grabbed me and pulled me out the door. She called Dad to get the gun. By the time Dad got to us the snake got out the chicken coop and was on the way under the smoke house. He shot the snake before it went completely under the smoke house.

Mom was trying to snap me out of my shock. She was talking to me, telling me everything was alright again and again. She put me in her arms and rocked me. After a while I was back to myself. The next day Sherry, Romeo and I went to the side of the smoke house. We saw blood and it looked like something was dragging down the cotton row.

The cotton field was next to the smoke house and after what we saw we knew that was the snake. A day or two later Dad went in the woods and found the snake dead, mouth wide open with the chicken still in it. Dad told us that because it had to move before it could close its mouth and was shot, its mouth couldn't close.

I'm so glad Mom felt something was wrong with me. I thank God for her. After all this, I would not go into a chicken coop by myself. Someone had to go with me.

Talking about snakes, I remember dad was planting corn and drawing rows for the corn to be planted when he plowed up a rattlesnake bed with lots of eggs. Dad stopped and got a stick and broke a few eggs finding rattlesnakes ready to hatch. When he saw this he gave Sherry, Romeo and me sticks to break up all the eggs.

After dad finished planting the corn and giving it time to grow, it was time to harvest the corn. The way to harvest corn is to break the corn from the stalk, put it in piles, come back later and pick it up putting the corn into the two horse wagon. Mom reached to pick up the corn and there was a big rattlesnake. Its head came up and it made a rattling sound. Mom didn't move. She called dad with a low voice a very, low voice. I don't know how he heard her but he did. He started coming toward her. She held up her hand and pointed toward the snake. Dad went back and got the gun and killed the rattlesnake. That snake had a lot of horny rings on its tail. Then mom moved away. She thought she was a goner that time.

Dad got a stick and picked up the snake finding a lot of eggs under her. Dad gave me, Sherry and Romeo sticks and told us to break up all the eggs. As we broke up the eggs we found there were some ready to hatch and we killed them all. We hacked them to death making sure there were none left.

Mom went and sat on the back of the wagon just to pull herself together. Mom said she was never so scared in her entire life. Dad went over and talked to her as she calmed down. After we finished we went home early and dad stopped planting corn in that field.

CHAPTER 6

Rifle and Gun

The next day when Dad got back from the store Mr. Whitehead came to talk to my parents about the big barn on the farm. Dad was using it to store hay and Mr. Whitehead wanted some of his other farmers to use it to store their hay. Dad said, "That's okay if we make rules." Mr. Whitehead and Dad agreed it would be ok as long as they were home. This was agreeable with Mr. Whitehead they shook hands and all was well for a while.

One day my parents went into town leaving us (the children) at home. Mr. Joe came by to get some hay.

My brother, Tyler, told him, "Mr. Joe you have to come back later because my mom and dad are not home."

Mr. Joe said, "I am not coming back, I am getting the hay now."

Tyler said, "Mr. Joe, no you are not!"

Mr. Joe said, "Who is going to stop me?"

Tyler said, "I am."

Tyler went and got his rifle and when he got back he told Mr. Joe, "If you take another step toward the barn, I will blow your damn head off."

Mr. Joe went and got Mr. Whitehead.

Mr. Whitehead told Mr. Joe, "Go ahead and get the hay."

Tyler said, "Oh no, you're not! If you don't want to get shot, stay the hell away from the barn. You two know the rules."

The two men looked at Tyler like they wanted to break his neck. They decided to wait for our parent to return.

When they got home, Dad asked Tyler why he had his rifle. Before he could say a word, Mr. Whitehead said, "Just a little misunderstanding. Everything is alright."

I wondered why Mr. Whitehead didn't raise hell with dad like he did with the other farmers.

Mom said, "That's why we have rules."

This wasn't the first time something like this happened. Sometime back Mr. Bill came to the house to get some hay. My brother, David, said, "Mr. Bill, Mom and Dad are not home you have to come back."

Mr. Bill said, "I don't have time to come back." He started toward the barn. David got my dad's gun.

David said, "If you take another step I will put a buck shot in your damn foot." Mr. Bill took another step toward the barn. David started shooting up in the air. Mr. Bill started running. He ran so fast he passed his truck. David kept shooting and Mr. Bill kept running. He ran all the way back to Mr. Whitehead's house.

When Mr. Bill got to Mr. Whitehead's house, he couldn't talk. When he was able to pull himself together he told Mr. Whitehead to send someone else for the truck.

Mr. Bill said, "I am not going back for the truck those children are crazy like their father."

I asked Mom why Mr. Bill said we were crazy. She said, "My children are not crazy they just know the rules." She didn't say a word about dad.

I thought Mr. Bill said that because dad got drunk on the weekends and some Monday's he had a hangover. On one of those Monday's Mr. Whitehead stopped by and asked my dad why he wasn't in the field working. He said, "You need to be out in the field."

Dad went off on Mr. Whitehead and said, "That was not the deal I made with you. I said I will give you the best crops and so far I've done what I said every year. What in the hell are you trying to do, tell me how to farm. Get the hell away from me and let me do the farming. As long as I am on top you don't need to say a damn word to me. When I stop being on top then you will have the right to say something to me about the crops. In the meantime keep your ass away from me."

Dad went back into the house and took the whole day off. Getting back into the truck Mr. Whitehead drove off laughing.

My dad was always nice to his family but when he was in his whisky he was another person.

Mom loved her little man and we loved him too. My brother David gave my dad the name 'little man' because he was five feet seven inches in height and weighed around 140 to 160 pounds. Mom was five feet eleven and weighed around 200 to 250 pounds. Through the hurt, pain, other women, no matter what—we still loved him.

"For better or worse," Mom said, "Your dad was and will always be the only man in my life." That was just how my mom and dad were. Now, I never said dad didn't have problems; he had lots of problems but we got over it.

Dad came home many times singing about his brown skin baby over and over. That's what he called my mom when he was drunk.

In our little town everyone knew every bodies business. Dad didn't care or give a damn what people thought or knew. When he came home from a night out, if he had had a good time with his woman, he would come home singing, get in his bed and go to sleep. If he had a bad time with one of his women he came home raising all kind of hell.

Sometimes he'd get the gun and run us all out of the house on those nights. If mom had enough time she would get some blankets for us to sleep on the side of the road until he'd go to sleep. Sometime it took Dad a long time to go to sleep. Sometimes before my brother got to him he would wake up and start shooting in the trees or wanting to fight with everyone. He couldn't fight all of us so he would give up and go to sleep.

In all of the time we were all together I only saw my dad hit my mom a few times and some of my siblings stopped him. We were tired of Dad's shit so Mom and Tyler went and got all of my dad's gun shells. We hid them so he couldn't find them, that's what we thought but my dad had a green box he kept locked. They over looked that box and we went to bed that night feeling good. We thought we had all the shells.

About twelve o'clock we heard a loud noise and jumped up to find dad had shot a big hole in the floor in the girl's room between the two beds; Dad was standing there holding the gun. Tyler took the gun away from him. Mom was so mad, she didn't say a word. We all went back to bed but didn't get very much sleep. The next morning Dad got up and fixed the floor.

After fixing the floor, Mom sat down with him and had a talk. She said, "One of these days you are going to kill someone else." At that time we didn't know what mom was talking about so we just over looked what she had said. Then she went on to say, "From that gun one of your son's is half blind in one eye because you didn't put your gun away after you came in from hunting and he looked down the barrel of the gun and got gun powder in his eye. Now you are shooting in the girl's room. One day you are going to kill one of us— me or your children."

That did something to Dad. He went and got the shells out of his green box and gave them all to mom. For a while everything was alright, he then wanted his shells back, we all said a big "NO! You are not going to get your shells back. You can only have them when you need them during the week. But no shells when you are drunk!"

Dad calmed down but the drinking and running around with his women didn't stop. He stopped shooting in the floor but he still ran around with his women while mom went to help others.

Mr. Sinclair, a friend of my parents whose niece lost her mother and father years ago had only her two children and her uncle that raised her.

Early one morning Mom and I were going into town getting the wagon ready to sell eggs and other things she was taking to another neighbor. Mom went back into the house to get something else when she spotted Mr. Sinclair coming down the road. When Mr. Sinclair got into the yard he said, "Good Morning" to us and we greeted him. He asked Mom if she would take something to his niece.

He said, "Her husband beat her up real bad and threatened to kill her. Lolar ran out the house with only what she had on, grabbed her two children and hitch hiked to my house."

Mr. Sinclair had put her in an old house he was taking care of for Mr. Newton's grandson. Old Newton died years ago. After he explained everything to the grandson, he said, "Lolar and her children could stay there as long as she wanted to." That was very nice of that white man.

Mr. Sinclair went to the store and got a few things for Lolar and her family. That's when he came to the house and asked Mom if she would take the things to his niece. He was afraid her husband Butch was following him and he didn't want to lead him to Lolar and the children. Mom told him, "Yes, I will take the things to Lolar."

Mr. Sinclair said, "If you can help out with any clothing, I will be very grateful."

Mom asked, "What size is she?"

He said, "About your size." He also told her the children's ages. Mom went back into the house and got two old dresses of hers and some clothes for the children and other things to add with what Mr. Sinclair had. She got blankets for them, grits, a piece of ham, meal, sweet potatoes, white potatoes and lots of other things plus medicine for Lolar. Then off we went to take them to Lolar.

We rode and rode, it seemed like we were never going to get there. I went with mom to a lot of places and was never afraid. This time I was afraid because we had to ride most of the time through the woods. I said to myself, "Please God let us get there soon."

After riding a little more we were finally there. Mom drove Nell, the mule, to the back of the house. We got out and Mom knocked on the door. "Mr. Sinclair sent me."

There was no answer. She knocked again and said the same thing. This time a tall lady came to the door. I said to myself, 'Oh my God she looks like a monster.' I was afraid of her. Butch had put a hurtin' on her. This is my daughter, little Barbara Ann McKay, and I am big Barbara Ann McKay, I named her after me.

She said, "I am Lolar Bell Windell and these are my children Paul and Holly." We shook hands and my mom and I went to take all the things out of the wagon. Mom took the wagon and Nell down in the woods and tied her to a tree. She walked back to the house. I was so afraid of Lolar. I was praying for Mom to hurry back when she walked in and then I was ok again.

Every time she heard a noise, Lolar jumped. It didn't matter if it was a big or small sound, she ran to the window. She did that for some time. She almost jumped out of her skin. It was still cold so she had a little fire to keep them warm. Mom went outside and got some wood and began putting pieces on the fire. Then she closed the door to the rooms and it was much warmer. Mom said, "If it gets too hot, open the door, if it gets too cold, close the door. Close the door one at a time if it gets too cold."

Mom wanted to calm Lolar down by telling her about her uncle and the things he had sent to her. Then Mom started looking around for some pots and pans. She cleaned them and cooked some food for all of us. She fixed us something to eat, then gave the kids and Lolar a sponge bath. She rubbed Lolar down with some Liniment, it burned a little but she was alright. They went to sleep for about three hours. When Lolar woke up my mom said, "We have to go now." I could see Lolar didn't want us to go home.

Mom said, "We will be back to check on you and the kids." And we did just that a few more times.

Lolar was still afraid. One day we all were outside cleaning up and Mr. Sinclair drove up to us. When we saw him, Mom and I were so afraid something bad had happened to Lolar and her children.

We waited for Mr. Sinclair to stop and start talking. He said, "I have good news and bad news."

Mom thought for a moment and replied, "Give me the bad news first."

He said, "Lolar's husband, Mr. Butch, is dead. Someone beat him to death."

Mom said, "Are you sure he is dead?"

Mr. Sinclair nodded and said, "He is *grave-yard* dead! The good news is that Lolar and the children can come out of hiding."

I said, "All of it is good news, they are free, thank God."

Lolar and her children came out of the woods and moved closer to her uncle. She put her little boy in school.

One day mom and I were in town selling eggs to Mr. and Mrs. Donnelly. We bumped into Lolar and her children. We hugged each other and were glad to see them. Lolar thanked us again for our help. They looked so happy and different. They were smiling and smiling like they had always been that way.

CHAPTER 7

The Green Family

We were all very happy about Lolar and her family. When we heard about the Green Family, mom, with her helping heart, was on another mission. She loved to help others if she could. It was so painful for the whole town. The Green Family was a lovely family, Mr. and Mrs. Green had eight children, four boys and four girls. The children were very close they were like stair-steps.

One day their house caught on fire. Mrs. Green realized her three-month-old baby was still in the house. She went back inside to get her baby. When she got to the door she threw her baby to her oldest son. She went through the floor and the house fell down on her. All that could be seen was fire and hear Mrs. Green screaming and hollering. It seemed that the sound would never end. Then she said, "O Lord God, have mercy on me," and she was gone.

The heart breaking part is that the children were watching their mother burning up in the fire. Mom said, "Lord have mercy on all of the Green Family." The entire township was in pain even some of the white people. I went to school with some of the Green children. I even liked one of the boys.

At the funeral I think everyone was crying. The children and their dad completely were crazy with grief. Neither he nor the children could be comforted at that moment. That was the most heart breaking funeral I'd ever seen. I am seventy-two now, and that funeral with the family still lingers in my memory.

As you know it was closed casket to lessen the grief of the family. I'm pretty sure that Mr. Green and the children would have tried to pull her out of the casket. He was falling on the casket and asking God "Why did you take my wife away from me and my children?" Some people walked out of the church because they couldn't take it.

Mrs. Green had been a good mother and wife and took good care of her family, now she was gone and things would all be different. After the funeral everything for the family went downhill. Mr. Green however, still brought the children to church but it was not the same. The girls needed their hair combed and the boys needed haircuts, clothes were not ironed along with other family needs.

It really hurt to know that no one wanted to give a helping hand to the family.

After church one Sunday, my mom walked up to Mr. Green and asked how he and the children were doing. He said, "Mrs. Barbara, we are not doing so well. I miss my wife so much, especially her biscuits."

Mom told him, "I will be there at your house tomorrow to show your little girls how to make biscuits."

The boys were older than the girls with the oldest girl being thirteen. Mom showed her how to make biscuits. Mom made one pan, then Doreen made a pan and they turned out good. She showed the children everything they needed to know.

After this incident I now had other children to play with. Most of my little life I was around older people but it sure felt good to have young people around. I liked going to the Green family's house. Whenever I went over I tried to make myself pretty because I liked one of the Green boys.

Mom called me about three times. When I didn't answer she said, "I'm not going to call you again." I ran and jumped in the wagon. Mom said, "What's that I smell? What do you have on?"

I said, "Nothing Mom." She asked me, "Do you think you're going to catch you a boyfriend?

"I might." She laughed and said OK you just might.

Every time we visited the Green Family they were so very happy to see us. Mom taught the children everything they needed to know in order for them to be comfortable. She explained to them the importance of helping each other. One of the boys said, "Dad doesn't like his boys doing house work."

The oldest one joined in saying, "I used to help Mom when Dad wasn't around."

Mom had a little talk with Mr. Green telling him it was alright for his boys to do house work. They will not turn out to be sissies. Mom told him that she had nine girls and three boys. The girls work just as hard as the boys side by side in the field and around the house. After having the talk with Mr. Green, the boys started helping to make life easier for the family.

Mrs. Green had a cookbook that she used and Mom showed the girls how to use it with good results. Each time she got better and better with the meals. One day while at church Mr. Green reported that his daughter could now make biscuits almost as good as his wife. Mom said, "Give her a little more time and she will be cooking and making biscuits *better* than your wife."

We went back a few more times, but Mom knew the children were ready to be on their own. If they needed something or had questions, they would ask her at church.

Now I was getting tired of the visits with my new family. I asked my mom, "Don't you think you've done enough for the Green family?"

Mom gave me a real mean look and said, "You shouldn't be jealous. The Green children don't have a mother but you do. Don't you like sharing your mother for this little while? I know that all the good we've done will come back to us later. The Green children can't get their mother back. Barbara Ann, you should be ashamed of yourself and ask God to stop you from thinking the way that you are. It is so much better to help people than be selfish."

This made me feel so, bad leaving me with nothing to say. I did what Mom suggested and I asked God to please help me not be selfish. It made me feel much better talking with my mom about this.

As Mom and I went to take some food to her brother, Uncle Bud and his family, Mom said, "On our way back we'll give the Green family a surprise visit." When we arrived at their house we were surprised to see how clean the house was. The children had learned very well now and the family was doing great. The children were glad to see us and they had smiles on their faces. Doreen surprised mom by baking some cookies and serving Coca Cola and we enjoyed both very much. Mom was really happy when we left because she felt the children were truly ok and no longer needed help.

Mrs. Bell, one of the elders, didn't like how close Mom was to the children. She was jealous of the relationship that my mom had built with the family. She told Mom, "If you keep being around the Green family they will bring your family down to their standards." I could tell that did not sit well with my mother.

Mom said, "Really? Just for helping?" Then she shook her head and said, "I don't think so," and walked away.

It was Easter Sunday when the Green family came to church looking real fine. Everyone was surprised to see how well the family was doing. The girls were beautifully dressed, hair combed, and the boys and Mr. Green were all handsomely dressed with nice haircuts. The family had come a long way from the day of the fire. The entire community was speechless.

Immediately, after church service and the end of the children's program, Mr. Green asked the pastor if he could say a few words. The pastor gave consent and Mr. Green rose from his seat and began by thanking the McKay family for all their help after his wife's death. "Mrs. Barbara was a life saver with all her children that she has, she still had time to help my children and me any way she could to get back on our feet. Mr. McKay, or Gil, he always found time to talk with me offering to help if I needed it."

Mr. Green then went on to say, "I couldn't leave little Barbara out because she was right there to help anyway she could. Always by her mother's side with showing my little girl how to comb her hair, put it in a ponytail, hang up her clothes and much, much more."

Mr. Green then said, "From the bottom of my heart, I really want to thank Mr. and Mrs. McKay and their family." He continued to say that some of the people he knew, old friends and others stopped speaking to him. If he said hello they would walk away. Those who he thought were his closest friends who were closer than the McKay family wouldn't speak to him. They never came over to help or ask if he needed help and he told them that it really hurt him. To go further he also said, "This really proved to me who my true friends were."

He finished by saying, "Thank you again McKay family for all that you've done for my family. I tell you this goes for my children as well, for some of them can remember the fire and others will never know about the fire unless someone tells them. They will never have the opportunity to know their mother. Their ages ranged from three months to three years old. So I say again to the McKay family you've really placed love feelings within my heart."

Several months later Mr. Green asked my mom about a lady named Beth. He wanted to know if she was a nice lady. Mom said, "Yes she is a very nice lady." Sometime later they were married. Immediately the little one's started calling her mommy and the oldest called her Mrs. Beth.

Members of the Green family were: Mr. Walter Green, Mrs. Beth Green, Donna, Dewitt, Dexter, David, Dale, Doreen, Daisy, and Dolly. The marriage of Mr. Walter and Mrs. Beth Green made the Green family a happy household again.

The McKay family truly believed that God put the right two people together healing the hurt and mending the broken hearts. Whenever you saw the family they were very happy. Mrs. Beth always gave Mr. Green and the children lots of love. In return they gave her the same loving feelings.

Now when everything had settled down, Mr. and Mrs. Green gave birth to a baby girl. Her name was Doris and my mom felt that this was a blessing from God in completing the healing and mending the brokenness of the family.

CHAPTER 8

Antoinette and Hilary

The Green family was now doing fine and no longer needed our help. We were now able to return to doing for ourselves.

My sister, Antoinette, wrote to our mom saying she and her girls were coming for a summer visit. She was the oldest sister. I really didn't know her that well. I saw her once when she came home after getting married. At that time she was doing very well and the only thing she said to the rest of us was "hello" when mom introduced her to all of us. I said to myself, "She is not my sister but she is very pretty." She left home before I was born and had only visited once before but this was the second visit.

My brother, David, left when I was about five years old. I vaguely remembered him. The last four of us children don't really remember either of them very well. However, every one of my siblings knew I was the mean one. It didn't take them long to understand that about me.

Antoinette and Hilary loved to call on me to do things for their children while they just sat around doing nothing. I would talk to my mom about this repeatedly but she just said "They're your older sisters and you have to listen to them." This made me extremely mad as hell.

One day everyone was sitting on the front porch with Hilary and her family and just visiting. She was sitting with her husband, Leon, with his head in her lap playing in his hair. Hilary, knowing her son, Parker, loved sweet potatoes would call me to get them for him. She would occasionally call the others but mostly she'd call me. I looked at mom, I could see it if Hilary was busy doing some work. The last time she called out to me, I gave Mom a mean look.

Mom said, "Sit back down."

Then mom said to Hilary, "You don't have a maid around here, get up and get things for your own children." Hilary didn't like that. I think Antoinette and Hilary were getting a kick out of telling me what to do.

Now mom turned the tables around and said, "If any of your sister's and brother's want to help out it's alright but they don't have to and you can't make them."

I could see hell rise up in Hilary's eyes. She tried to get mom to change her mind. Both of them were not happy with what mom said and tried repeatedly to get her to change her mind. Mom however, stuck to her guns saying, "They're *your* children! How would you like it if your young children had to wait on the older ones?" This stopped them from asking mom to change her mind.

Don't get me wrong. It's not that I didn't want to do for my sister's. No, that wasn't it! It was just that they were sitting on their asses and doing nothing. I didn't mind helping out if they were busy; but they weren't and I was jumping up and down doing what they should have been doing for their children. I was now free and they couldn't make me do anything else.

Now Antoinette decided I was going to do what she said when Mom and Dad weren't around. She asked me to take her little girl, Sandras' potty outside and clean it out. I said, "No that's your job you clean it out. You can't make me do it."

Boy, she was mad as hell, so she asked Romeo to do it and he did. She gave him a dime. Back then, that was a lot of money and she thought that hurt me. Let me tell you, it didn't.

When Dad got home I told him that Romeo had a dime so Dad gave me a dime also. After supper, I got right in front of Antoinette and started playing with my dime. She told mom I took Romeo's dime. Mom asked me where I got my dime from. I said, "From Dad." Mom said to Antoinette, "That's not Romeo's dime." She thought Mom was going to take mine from me.

The next day at supper time she asked Romeo what he did with his dime. He went into the room to find the dime and couldn't. Antoinette said, "I know you took his dime."

Dad said, "No I gave little Barbara a dime." Everyone started looking at each other wondering who was telling the truth. No one said a word. Then Romeo felt in his pocket and there was the dime. I looked at Antoinette and smiled. This made her twice as mad and really there was nothing she could do about it—*well, that's what I thought.*

The following day Mom and Dad went shopping for food. They left Lucille in charge of us until they returned. Mom told Sherry and I to sweep the yard. Sherry and I started fighting over a pair of yard brooms. She said, "They were hers."

I came right back at her and said, "They're not yours they belong to me."

Before Lucille could get to us Antoinette, ran out of the house and slapped Sherry. She left all five of her finger prints on Sherry's face. Then she started toward me. I ran to the wood pile and grabbed the axe. I told Antoinette, "If you slap me, or put your hands on me I will chop you up like mincemeat and feed you to the damn hogs! Before I let you slap me like that, I will kill your ass. Come on big sister and slap me, let me see what you can do. Come on Nettie, let's see who's the boss."

I was swinging the axe back and forth. I could see she was afraid of me. At that time, I was about nine or ten years old. I said, "Come on let me make mincemeat out of you. Come on Bitch, come slap me."

Antoinette said, "You are crazy like your daddy."

I stayed out of sight waiting for Mom and Dad to come home. I started chopping on a piece of wood thinking it was Antoinette. She came to the door and said again, "You are crazy like your daddy."

I told her, "Dad is your Dad too. You look more like him than any of us." I said, "Come on big sister let me show you crazy just how crazy I really am."

She went back into the house.

Lucille was putting some ice on Sherry's face to keep the swelling down. I walked toward the highway and when I got there, I sat by the side of the road with my axe in my hand. Just then I heard Mom and Dad coming back. I was glad to see them. When they got to me, they stopped the truck and I got in with my axe. Dad pulled up in the yard and my mom asked me, "What's wrong? Why do you have the axe?"

I told Mom and Dad what happened, that Antoinette slapped Sherry and was trying to do the same thing to me. Mom got out of the truck and called Sherry. Mom said, "Let me see your face." The swelling had gone down some, but Antoinette's finger prints were still visible on Sherry's face.

Mom asked Lucille, "Why didn't you take care of the problem?

She said, "Antoinette got to them before I could."

Mom said, "I left Lucille in charge and you know that."

Antoinette said, "I took care of it, Mom."

Mom said, "No you didn't, Lucille doesn't hit them. That's Gilbert's and my job, not yours."

Then mom said, "Why did you slap one and not the other?"

She didn't know what to say. She didn't want mom to know she was afraid of me with the axe.

Then Mom turned to me and asked, "What were you going to do with the axe?"

I said, "If she slapped me like that, I was going to chop her up in little pieces and feed her to the pigs."

Mom said, "You wouldn't do that to you sister."

I said, "Yes, I would."

Mom said to Antoinette, "How would you like it if I did that to your little girls or if Sherry did that to them? You wouldn't like it would you?"

She didn't say a word. Then I told Dad what she said about me being crazy like him.

She didn't want me to say that and turned a Bluish Red. Dad looked right in her eyes and walked out the door.

Mom said to Antoinette, "That was wrong, what you did. Don't ever touch my children again, *never* again."

She was supposed to stay for the summer but only stayed three weeks. That happened on Friday and she left on Monday. I was glad to see her go. One nice thing I could say about Antoinette was that she was very beautiful, the prettiest of all of us. I'll give her that. She featured our dad. He was a very handsome man and that's why the women were always after him.

After hearing what Antoinette said about him, about me being crazy just like him, dad went out and got drunk. He made a circle around seven pecan trees like a snake. He really didn't like what she had said but he got over it. I must admit that I was really a little crazy and very much like my dad. I didn't favor him in looks like she did because I resembled my mom enough to be her twin. It was an astonishing resemblance but I made it work.

After Antoinette left things went back to normal.

CHAPTER 9

Little Barbara and Scott

It seems that *crazy* ran in the family. Mom was not too far behind the line of crazy. She always told us not to start a fight with people and she didn't like bullies picking on other children. She knew only one of her last four children would fight, and of course that was me.

There was a little, white boy named Scott, who lived down the street. He was a bad ass and we walked to and from school together. Scott rode his bike and when Tyler was walking with us there was no trouble. When Tyler started attending high school, the trouble began because he would pick on Sherry and me. He threw big old rocks at us.

Mom talked to his mom about what was going on. The next day he continued right on doing the same thing and it went on for about three more weeks. Mom kept telling Scotts' mom and instead of things getting better, they got worse.

Scott became sick with a very bad cold and rode his bicycle close to Sherry spitting in her hair. It was nasty blue, green and black stuff from his cold. I tried getting that shit out of her hair. It looked worse than shit. Most of it came out when we got home and mom got the rest.

Mom went to talk with Mrs. Dottie again. This time she was steaming mad and knew that nothing was going to be done

I said to Sherry, "Mrs. Dottie is not going to do anything to Scott but I know someone who will."

At that moment I remember what my brother, Tyler, said to me about leverage.

The next day the same thing happened again. I cleaned all that disgusting stuff out of Sherry's hair and told her not to tell mom anything about what happened. I've got something for him. I kept thinking about what Tyler told me about leverage. He told me I needed some leverage because I was so small.

He said, "I'm going away to work and I need to teach you how to take care of your sisters and brothers after I go." He continued, "You are the only one that will fight on a dime."

I wasn't afraid and he said, "Look for something to help you like a stick, bush, limb or rock whatever you can find."

The next day on our way to school I put whatever I could find on the side of the road. Scott was a bad dude and a pain in my ass but *this* time I was ready for him.

I told Sherry to walk behind me and I walked off the road a little. Scott was coming down the road as always and spat in Sherry's hair again and then he took off. He looked back, laughing his ass off at what he had done to Sherry. The very next time he looked back I walked back to the highway and grabbed Scott pulling him off his bicycle and it rolled down the highway and fell.

Now I had Scott where I wanted him. I beat the snot out of him. Snot was running out his nose. I beat him until he was red, white, and blue. I beat Scott with everything I could get my hands on. I had him down on the ground and said to Sherry, "Spit on his head and in his hair." She wouldn't do it.

At that time I had a bad cold too and spit that old blue, green and dark crap from my lungs in his hair. He was crying and crying

I yelled at him, "Shut the hell up! It doesn't feel good when the shoe is on the other foot does it?" I let him go. He jumped up got on his bicycle and away he went. By the time we got home Scott and Mrs. Dottie came speeding to the house.

She said to mom, "Barbara I know my Scott is bad, if it was one of your girls that beat his ass that was O.K. with me, but not the two of them

Mom said, "What are you talking about?"

Mrs. Dottie said, "Scott told me the girls double teamed him and beat him up like that."

Mom said, "Well, Mrs. Dottie, that just isn't true, only little Barbara beat his little bad ass."

Mrs. Dottie said, "That little girl couldn't beat my Scott like that all by herself? She is too small."

Mom said, "Small or not, she beat him. I know my children and what they will or will not do."

They were going back and forth getting madder and madder. I knew I had to do something. Scott was sitting in the truck. I eased up to the truck and said to Scott, "If you don't tell your mom the truth I will beat your ass tomorrow the same way."

Scott jumped out of the truck and ran to his mother and said, "It wasn't Sherry, only little Barbara who beat me up.

Mrs. Dottie said as she pointed toward me, "Boy you let *that* little gal beat your ass like that?"

Mrs. Dottie grabbed Scott by his ear and pulled him to her truck, then said, "Boy you make me sick!"

She said to mom, "Barbara I am so sorry, forgive me please."

She shoved Scott in the truck and said, "You make me ashamed of you." Her anger could be heard as she yelled, "Stay in the truck."

He tried to get out and Mrs. Dottie said, "Keep your ass in *this* truck, until I make up my mind about what I'm going to do to you." She sat quietly fuming and then said, "Boy, the whipping I'm gonna put on you will last for the rest of your life."

Scott learned his lesson and we didn't have any more trouble with Scott.

After the incident Scott stayed the hell away from us. On the way to and from school Scott would never pass by us, if he got close to us he would turn around and go another way.

If I'd known an ass whipping worked that well, I'd have done it much sooner. We had no more problems with Scott—*at all*.

Chapter 10

Dad and Mrs. Gladys

After what happened with Scott I didn't want to think that one of Dad's women would act up worse. I really didn't think Mrs. Gladys had similarities with Mrs. Ginny. Like mom always said, "You can't judge a book by its cover and what goes around would come around."

Mrs. Gladys used to stay in the background, she didn't come looking for Dad like Mrs. Ginny did but she would wait for him to come to her. Besides she was much older and no one talked much about her and my Dad. We sometimes heard that she and Dad had been fighting.

One day dad stopped by to see her and another man was there. Dad didn't like that and they started arguing. Dad ran the man away from Mrs. Gladys house. The two of them started arguing again. As the other man, Mr. Lee, was leaving he said to Mrs. Gladys, "See you later," and left.

Dad and Mrs. Gladys started fighting and Dad beat her up real bad, she was black and blue. Mrs. Gladys grandsons, Tim and Tan, didn't like what happened to their grandma. I guess it was time for Dad to get what he'd been dishing out. The other shoe had now fallen and Mrs. Gladys grandsons weren't having it.

Gladys and her grandsons set Dad up. They told Dad that Mrs. Gladys wanted to see him. Dad was feeling bad about what he'd done to her. He said, "Oh my God that woman must really love me especially after what I've done to her. I can't believe that she wants to see me."

In my mind I wanted to tell my father, "No Dad, she doesn't want to see you not the way you think. She wants to get even with you. She will make you sorry and her grandsons are going to help."

Dad was so glad Mrs. Gladys wanted to see him that he ignored my warning and went straight over to see what she wanted. He should have realized something was up. In past situations, it took almost two months before she would let him back into her life. Now it had only taken two weeks. Dad thought she was that much in love with him but little did he know what lay ahead for him.

When he got there, Mrs. Gladys was so nice and loving to him. They were kissing and hugging with strong passion like never before. She was pouring it on heavy and they finally started making passionate love together. Dad said it was the best sex he'd ever had beside Mom's. You didn't have to ask Dad what he was doing on the weekends with his women because he would tell all about it.

Suddenly she stopped and said, "I don't want no more."

Dad said he was in another world. He let his temper get the best of him and said, "If you don't finish this I will beat the hell out of you again."

When he got those words out something hit him up side his head. He said, "It felt like a baseball bat and knocked him off the bed." He saw Mrs. Gladys and her grandsons and they started beating the hell out of him. They beat him really bad and someone hit him in the head again and knocked him completely out.

When he came to, he was rolled up inside an old moving blanket and stashed somewhere in an old house. The pain was unbearable. He couldn't move and just stayed there. The only thing he could do was pray. Yes, my Dad did knew how to pray. The only thing he could do was pray to be found.

When Dad didn't come home we were worried. After two days and no sign or word from Dad, then Mom, Tyler, Grandpa, Uncle Bud and a few friends went looking for him. They looked for about a week and a half with no luck. Mom was beginning to think they would never find him. They were asking everyone they knew if anyone had seen him. No one had any news.

Uncle Bud saw Mrs. Gladys while he was on his way home and asked if she had seen dad, and she shook her head and said, "No!"

The next day my friend Cude came to play with me. I was so worried about my dad that I didn't want to play so I asked Mom if I could walk her half way home. Mom said that would be fine. When we were a little way from the house, Cude told me where my dad was. She said, "He's in an old house in Murray Woods.

I asked her, "How do you know?"

She replied, "I heard my aunt, Gladys, talking to her grandsons." Yes, my friend was Dad's girlfriend's niece. Mom knew this but it didn't stop us from being friends. She said, "It's not the children's fault what the older people do."

Cude told me her aunt and her grandsons were talking about Dad. They were saying he must be dead by now. I told Cude I'd have to walk with her another time. I had to catch Mom and Tyler before they went out again looking for Dad.

I started running real fast because I had to get back to the house before they left again looking for my Dad. I didn't know I could run that fast. I just had to get to them before they left that's what I kept telling myself over and over. When I got to the dirt road, I was almost out of breath and had to stop, I couldn't run anymore. I thought I had missed them and sat by the road trying to get myself together. I looked up and they were coming down the dirt road toward me to get to the highway.

I was glad to see them. Mom said, "Take a deep breath." I did and began to tell Mom what Cude had said about Murray Woods. They broke his arm, cracked three of his ribs, fractured his legs and he has a concussion with a lot of other things wrong. Mom asked, "How did Cude know?"

I said, "Crude's aunt, Mrs. Gladys, and her grandsons beat him up and put him in that old house to die. Mom kept asking me questions.

Grandpa finally said, "Barbara, stop asking her questions. Let's go!"

Then mom asked, "Are you *sure* that's what she said?"

Grandpa questioned my mom, "Why not there?" Grandpa told me to go home and get a glass of water and put a little vinegar in it and drink it. He said, "Just a little."

Mom wanted to ask me more questions but Grandpa stopped her and said to Tyler, "Go!" And away they went. It took them about half an hour to get there. I went home and did what Grandpa told me to do. I drank the water and vinegar and felt a lot better. I was praying they would find Dad.

When they got to the old house, they called and called Dad with no answer. "Gil! Gil!" They called over and over but there was no answer.

One of them said, "Maybe he's not in there." Mom then put her ear to the door. She heard something moving and said, "He's in there!" They broke down the door and kept calling. Once inside the house the smell was bad. They thought it was a dead rat but looked further. As they move further into the house they heard a tap, tap, tap, and followed the tap and the smell which lead them to Dad. He was still alive, thank God! Boy did he stink! They had to cover their noses with their hands because it smelled like something was dead.

They rolled him in another blanket and put him in the back of the truck. Mom got in the back with him. When they got home she wouldn't let us see him until they (Mom, Tyler and Grandpa) cleaned him up.

We had to wait and I didn't want to wait. I wanted to see my Dad right then. I eased my little ass around to the back of the barn house where they were cleaning him up and peeked in a little hole. I got the shock of my life. My Dad looked like a monster. He scared me so bad. I eased my little ass from back there. When they'd finished cleaning him up, they took him to the house. Mom said, "Now you children can see your Dad."

My siblings went in to see him. I thought he looked the same and said, "No I don't want to see him." Mom had a little talk with me. She knew I had peeped in the barn. She said, "Dad looks much better." I then went in to see him. Mom was so right. He looked much better

My siblings were just looking not saying one word. I started talking and asked Dad what happened to him. He said, "I will tell you later." He couldn't talk very well.

I spoke kindly to him, "You don't have to talk. I will tell you what happened."

He said, "Tell me then."

I told him about what Mrs. Gladys and her grandsons had done to him. I said, "Daddy they were going to kill you. They want you dead, graveyard dead! You need to stay away from those people. One day they will kill you. I told him, "If they hurt you again, I will kill them when I grow up." I will beat the hell out of them.

Mom looked at me and said, "Watch your mouth."

"I'm sorry Mom, I was only thinking of Dad." Mom was not the only one who loved this little man, we loved him too.

Then Dad said to me, "When I get better you won't have to do anything. I will take care of them."

Dad was in town, he saw Mrs. Gladys and she wanted Dad to come back to her. He looked her in her eyes and said, "What I did to you wasn't right and I'm sorry, but what you and your grandsons tried to do to me by leaving me for dead wasn't right either. If it had been just an ass whipping I could have forgiven you, but you all tried to kill me and when they asked if you'd seen me you said "No!" I would never think of coming back to you.

Approximately four months after what they'd done to my Dad, Mrs. Gladys was begging Dad to take her back. She said, "Please, please, please!"

Dad continued to say "No."

She grabbed Dad and got on her knees begging and begging him to take her back. He pushed her away and said, "Hell no. I will not ever have anything to do with you, never, never again." He walked away.

Mrs. Gladys said, "I guess I'll have to work on getting one of your sons." Dad almost lost it but kept his cool and said, "My sons don't want your old ass." Dad said, "Find your old ass another fool." I didn't think Dad would get away from Mrs. Gladys, but he did and we love him for that.

CHAPTER 11

Little Barbara and the Teacher

Although I was taught to love everybody, there were times my heart wouldn't let me. There was a girl whose name was Joslene and we went to school together and sometimes even had lunch together but other times we didn't. On one occasion my siblings and I decided to go into the woods hunting rabbits, low and behold we caught two. After skinning and cleaning the rabbits we cooked and took them for our lunch. The rabbits lasted for about a week. Mom made her yeast biscuits and for that week we shared lunch together. My friend Joslene saw us with our lunch and wanted some I gave her almost half but that didn't seem to be enough for her because she wanted more. I told her if I gave her more then I wouldn't have enough for myself. She slapped the sandwich out of my hand. I was quite surprised and we ended up fighting.

Joslene beat the hell out of me. There was no time to look for anything to use as leverage as Tyler had said to do. Joslene was a big girl, I tried fighting back but I was no match for her. As they watched the fight the other children were laughing and chanting, "Fight, fight, fight, fight."

We were in the school yard and Mrs. Conway my teacher was asleep at her desk. When she heard the noise she jumped up and ran outside. Asking no questions, she grabbed me and pulled me into the little school room.

Everyone wanted to know why she grabbed me, why she didn't grab Joslene who started the fight? Then Mrs. Conway said, "You McKay children are always in trouble." She shoved me down on the bench and started hitting my head on the bench. My brother Tyler tried to get to me to stop Mrs. Conway from hitting my head on the bench, but his friends didn't want him to get in trouble so they stopped him.

I asked her why she was hitting my head on the bench and she didn't answer me. She just kept on hitting my head again and again. Joslene was outside laughing her ass off at what was happening to me.

The next time Mrs. Conway hit my head on the bench I jumped up and slapped the snot out her nose. She was so surprised I didn't know what happened to me, I guess I lost my mind for a few minutes. Mrs. Conway said, "I'm taking you home." On our way to my house she passed my sibling and didn't give them a ride. I wondered why and later found out.

When Mrs. Conway got to the house she started telling mom all sort of lies, that's why she didn't stop and give them a ride because she didn't want my siblings there. I knew and she knew they would tell my mom the truth.

My teacher said, "She pushed me and then slapped me."

Mom said, "Why did Barbara push and slap you?"

Mrs. Conway said, "They were fighting."

Mom said, "Who was fighting?"

Mrs. Conway said, "I didn't know. I didn't ask any questions about those involved or why they were fighting."

My sister Hilary was visiting from up North and said, "The reason you don't know what happened is because you are always sleeping every day during lunch and the children throw popcorn up your dress while your legs are wide open. How I know this is because you were my teacher too."

Mom said, "Hilary you need to go into the house."

Mom said to Mrs. Conway, "I will take care of what Barbara did so you can go home now."

She said, "You are not going to beat her?"

Mom said, "I will make up my mind when my other children get home. Maybe they can explain what happened better than what you're telling me. I will wait for them."

Then Hilary said, "If you were paying more attention to the children you're supposed to be teaching you would know what was going on."

Mrs. Conway was mad and left.

I thought mom and dad were going to beat me black and blue I was just waiting. Of course hitting the teacher was a bad thing and I knew that already. Mom told me to sit on the porch until the other children came home. She kept asking me what happened repeatedly. When the others finally arrived mom asked them over and over what had happened. They told her the same thing I'd said to her.

Mom began feeling my head and found a lot of knots in my head. She said, "I am not going to beat you this time. You've been beat up enough."

Mom said, "Mrs. Conway wasn't fair about the fight."

I said, "Thank you God, I wasn't getting a whipping or beating.

The next morning I went to school and Mrs. Conway asked me if I needed a pillow.

Tyler said, "No she didn't get a whipping or a beating. My mom saw through your world of lies." After school, Tyler went to Joslene and told her, "If you ever put your hands on my sister again, I am going to beat your fat ass."

Joslene thought she could beat Tyler like she had beaten me. While he was talking to her, she shoved him and told him, "You go to hell!" That's all Tyler wanted Joslene to do and he began putting a hurting on her big ass. She didn't come to school for two days. When she came back she wanted to talk to me. Tyler said, "I told you to stay away from my sister or I will beat your ass again. I guess she didn't want that ass whipping anymore so she stopped messing with me.

Mom and I thought we had finished with what had been done but Mrs. Conway decided to punish me further by making me repeat the fourth grade. I was so angry I cried all the way home that day. Mom and I went back to school and asked Mrs. Conway why I was repeating the fourth grade.

Mrs. Conway said, "Her grades dropped at the end of the school year."

Mom said, "Why you didn't tell me her grades were dropping? You didn't let me know she was having a problem."

Mrs. Conway said to mom, "You can't help her."

Mom asked, "Why not?"

Mrs. Conway said, "Because you only completed the sixth grade."

Mom said, "This is the fourth grade! Who do you think was helping her get this far?"

Mrs. Conway said, "No wonder she got bad grades!"

Mom thought to herself, let me get the hell away from here before I break every bone in her body.

Mom said, "This is not the end of this conversation." She walked out of the little school house madder than a wet hen.

The following year a new school was built by the government for the black children. We were able to then ride the bus instead of walking.

As things progressed the next year, I had a male teacher Mr. London, who asked why I was repeating the fourth grade. I explained what had happened and he gave me a placement test for the fifth grade. This test was given by Mr. Garfield, the principal, and Mr. London.

Following the test and passing I was automatically placed in the fifth grade, I was sent to Mrs. Conway who was now teaching fifth grade.

When I walked into her class she said, "What are you doing here?"

I said, "I was given a test and after passing was placed in your class."

Mrs. Conway turned blue. She didn't know what to do or say. Then she said, "Take a seat." I remained in her class and she acted as if I wasn't even there.

Two weeks later I went to the principal and asked him if I could transfer to another class. Mr. Garfield asked why and I told him Mrs. Conway doesn't talk to me. When she is teaching and she asks a question, I raise my hand to answer and she completely ignores me. She will not call on me or recognize my hand up.

After I requested a transfer, Mr. Garfield, Mr. London, Mrs. Conway and I had a meeting in the principal's office. Mr. Garfield told Mrs. Conway, "What you did to Barbara and her mother wasn't right."

The principal asked me, "What do you want Mrs. Conway to do besides saying she's sorry?

I said, "I want her to write, *I'm sorry* 1000 times."

Mr. Garfield said to Mrs. Conway, "If you don't do what little Barbara is asking you to do as the punishment, I will take you before the school board where you may get suspended for about one month or more." He said, "Take your pick Mrs. Conway." She chose to do the writing assignment.

I asked the principal if I could say a few words to Mrs. Conway.

He answered yes. I told Mrs. Conway, "You see, what goes around comes around." I smiled at her for all the hell she'd put mom and me through and we had the last laugh. "You tried to make my mom and me feel and look like we were dumb. Now who looks dumb? Mrs. Conway, who looks like a dumb fool? You!" The principal transferred me to his class and everything was remarkably different.

CHAPTER 12

Mom and Dad's Liquor Store

As time went by Mom and Dad decided to make corn beer and wine. Mom thought this would keep Dad home more, but it didn't work. Dad would bring his friends over to drink at home and then disappear and go off to see his other women.

When his friends came over to drink with him and he wasn't home, they still wanted to drink. Dad not being home made no difference to his friends. That didn't stop them from coming over and mom decided to start selling the beer and wine. They called the wine Sue Cat. Mom soon graduated from the wine and beer to moonshine. She would get a gallon of moonshine and put it in half pint bottles and on the weekends we had all kind of company stopping by to drink.

There is always one asshole in the bunch. Mr. Ward kept getting whisky on credit; not paying and racking up a bill. He told mom he would pay her next week and next week never came. After the third time mom said, "No more credit, Mr. Ward." This made him mad and he told the police about Mom selling moonshine. Mr. Frank, a friend of Mr. Wards, came and told my mom what Mr. Ward had done. Mom told Tyler to take the moonshine in the woods, dig a hole and bury it.

Mom wasn't worried about the beer and wine because she could explain that it was fine to make beer and wine in her own house for her family, but not moonshine.

By the time Tyler got back, and not a minute too soon, the police arrived. They asked Mom if is she was selling moonshine and she said, "No!" The police then asked why so many people were around her house. Mom said, "Some of the people around the house were her husband's drinking buddies. They would bring their own bottles and drink with Dad from time to time. She said, "They can't drink in the street so they come over and drink with Gil.

Mom asked them if they wanted to talk to Dad right away and they said, "No it's alright." They had had so many run in's with Dad but they couldn't do anything to him because Mr. Whitehead told them to leave Dad alone. That's how much pull he had in the town.

The last time they had a run in with Dad was when he was driving too fast and they stopped him giving him a ticket. Dad said, "You better give me another one I'm coming back doing the same damn thing." That's when Mr. Whitehead stopped the police from messing with Dad. He would cuss them out and walk away. They already knew from Mr. Whitehead not to bother Dad and they decided not to talk with him.

Mom knew what Mr. Whitehead had told the police about Dad and they kept moving on. The police again asked about the moonshine. She told them, "No, no moonshine here."

Mom told the police, "I sell some things."

I said to myself, "Oh hell, Mom, why did you say that? You're going to jail." They were surprised to hear mom say she did sell.

The police said, "What do you sell?"

Mom said, "Vegetables of all kind, watermelons and peanuts. Would you like to buy some?"

The police said, "Yes two watermelons and two pecks of peanuts."

They looked around and asked my mom, "Where are the watermelons and peanuts?"

Mom said, 'They're in the field right now but if you come back in about one hour, you'll get some juicy watermelons and peanuts." They came back in forty-five minutes, paid Mom and left. When they were out of sight we all had a big laugh.

My brother, Tyler, said, "Mom you can sell the police the Brooklyn Bridge." Mom did a lot of things to make ends meet. One thing I *can* say, she didn't drink beer, wine, or whiskey.

Dad drank enough for the two of them together. Mom had two little helpers Sherry and Romeo. They loved helping mom strain the beer and wine. When they had finished straining, they were now ready to rest. There were times when I helped with the process and bottled the beer and wine.

One day I asked my mom why she told the police she only sold vegetables, peanuts and watermelons. She said, "Whenever they pass the house and see a lot of people here they will think I'm selling vegetables and I didn't want them to stop here anymore."

After a few more times, the police drove by the house just to see if mom was selling anything other than vegetables, watermelons and peanuts. Mom and Dad worked very hard to have the best garden and crops for sale.

CHAPTER 13

Dad and the Mule, Red

In order for Dad to have the best crops, he needed Red and Nell, the mules. Nell looked like a mule, but Red looked like a horse. Everything Dad would tell Nell to do he had no trouble but when he would tell Red, this mule had a mind of its own. Sometime he would listen and other times he was just stubborn.

Dad knew how to get Red to listen and after Dad gave him a good whipping, there was no more trouble out of Red. Dad would clean Red up and ride into town and other places he visited on their way home. When Dad would get so drunk he couldn't drive the wagon, he would tie the rope on a stick attached to the side of the wagon and get in the back and tell Red to take him home. My father would fall asleep in the wagon and Red would make his way straight to the front door.

Red would make all kinds of noise so we would wake up and know Dad was home. Sometimes when no one came to get him, Dad would just sleep in the wagon or wake himself up. No matter how much Dad was drinking he would always put Red in his stall.

One night Dad and Red were on their way home and nearing the graveyard they heard some noise in the wagon wheel. Red started acting funny and Dad had a hard time controlling him. This would happen every time Dad and Red passed the graveyard and after they passed the graveyard the noise stopped.

One day Dad was talking to Mom and Grandpa Edgar who was a reader and healer. He told Dad, "Pour some whisky on the wagon wheel."

Dad asked Grandpa Edgar, "Why?"

Grandpa said, "There's a white man in the grave yard and he wants a drink so give him a little."

The next time Dad heard that noise he did exactly what Grandpa told him and the noise stopped. If he didn't have any whisky he didn't hear any noise but when he had whiskey, then the noise would start again.

Dad said to Grandpa, "Why the hell does he want *my* whisky? I'm black and he's white."

That's a white graveyard," said Grandpa.

Grandpa said, "That dead, white man don't care what color you are as long as he gets his whisky." Back in those days the white man was something else. They tried to talk to you any kind of way.

Mr. Whitehead tried that with Dad and Dad told him "Hell no, if you want me to work for you, you're going to talk to me the right way."

Each time Mr. Whitehead spoke to Dad the wrong way he would cuss him out. After the cussing, Mr. Whitehead didn't bother Dad because he was the best farmer and was bringing him a lot of money with the cotton. The money was to be split half and half but of course he didn't split the profits he received from the pictures he took of the cotton field, corn and my mom's garden with Dad.

When you see a cotton field in a book it could be my dad's cotton. He had the best cotton and corn in the whole south and that's why Mr. Whitehead kept telling Dad lies to keep him in debt. That man was a good liar from the bottom of his heart. Every year Dad thought he was out of debt Mr. Whitehead put him right back in debt with his lies and I.O.U's. Dad always believed him, so Mr. Whitehead let him do whatever he wanted.

After cotton picking time, there were little scraps of cotton left in the field. Mom asked Mr. Whitehead if we could have the scraps and he said, "Yes." We needed the money for camp meeting. After we completed picking the scraps of cotton in the field, Mom and Tyler took the cotton to the gin. They received quite a bit of money from the scraps and when Mr. Whitehead saw how much they were making, he told Mom that he couldn't let her have the bail of cotton by herself.

He said, "I need half of the money that your husband, Gil, owes me so he took what he said Dad owed out of what they made from the scraps. There was only five dollars left.

Mom was mad as hell! She wanted to pop his eyes out of his head. When Mom and Tyler came home, they told us what Mr. Whitehead had done and that we couldn't go to camp meeting. We were so hurt and really didn't know what to do at that point. Mom prayed and prayed and we all joined in. She asked Dad if he had any money. Dad said, "No."

The next week Dad was running around with his friend, Mr. Rex. He stopped by the house to get something out of his little green box. In his rush, he forgot and left it open. I looked and saw the box wasn't locked, peeking in I saw twenty dollars and continued looking finding another five dollars. I told Sherry and Romeo about the money. We found my mom and told her about the money.

She said, "Lock it back up."

Sherry, Romeo and I said to Mom, "It's not fair, we work hard too, and Dad takes the money and runs around with his women.

That did it! Mom said, "Look in that box again."

We found another ten dollars in an old sock. We took twenty and left Dad fifteen and gave the money to Mom and we now had twenty five dollars between us.

Sherry went to the mail box finding a letter from Hope, our sister, with twenty-five dollars. Wow, we now had enough for camp meeting and there was still a week left. Tyler always had a little job and he would help Mom with what he made.

We found a few small jobs picking pecans, racking yards, or whatever we could find to do for some spending money. I didn't like to work in the fields but for camp meeting, I would work as hard as I could because I loved to go to camp meeting.

This was our little camp out for a week, no work, living in the woods with tents and gatherings with other farmers. This was our time to give thanks to God for a very productive year and making it through all the difficulties we had.

During the night we would make a big fire in front of our tents and sit around talking and laughing with each other. There was a big tent in the middle we called *The Church*. We had a chance to walk around, go to church meetings all day and the early part of the night. We met people from all over who came to camp meeting. Many different churches would meet during camp meeting to serve together. On the weekend there was always something planned at the big church tent so we were all working to make sure we had enough money for spending.

Mom had a job as well doing housework for Mr. and Mrs. Donnelly every now and then when they needed help. Two weeks before camp meeting, Mrs. Donnelly asked my mom to help her clean out her store because she was getting ready for a new shipment of food, clothes, shoes and other items to sell. When Mrs. Donnelly came to get Mom, her little girl, Betty, asked her mother if I could come with them to play. Her mother asked mom if it would be alright with her. Mom said, "Its okay."

When we arrived at her house she asked mom if she would like some used clothes for her children and Mom said, "Yes all I can get." Mrs. Donnelly said, "I wish I would have known before I threw out all those other clothes I had. She said Mrs. Olivia, who worked with her before Mom, didn't want any used clothes and I thought you were the same way.

Mom said, "I am not that way I'll use everything you give me for my children.

Mrs. Donnelly went and got a big box and started putting things in the box. She kept asking Mom if she could use this or that and Mom never said no to anything she received.

Mrs. Donnelly stopped asking and kept putting clothes and other items in the box. The things she was putting in the box looked new to me. When we got to the store she went crazy putting clothes and other items in the box.

Mrs. Donnelly's house and store were all together and while Mom was cleaning Mrs. Donnelly continued filling the boxes with different items. She paid Mom ten dollars which was a lot of money during those days.

When it was time to go home we found the box was too big to get in her car.

Mom said, "I'll get Gil to come back and get the box." She thanked Mom repeatedly and we went home.

After we arrived home, Mom told Dad about the things Mrs. Donnelly had put in the box for us and that he needed to get the truck to pick up the box she had for us, however when we returned there were three boxes. When Mom and Dad returned to the Donnelly's her husband was there and I said to myself I don't think he's going to let her give us all those things or maybe he thought the things Ms. Betty was putting in the boxes were really for their little daughter whose name was also Betty.

Mr. Donnelly said to Dad, "Back up to the door, I have a surprise for the family. There was another big box of clothing and one full of shoes, some new and some used. There was something in those boxes for everyone in our family.

The Donnelly's had the same number of children that Mom and Dad had at that time, three girls and two boys which all wore about the same size clothing. Mom and Mrs. Donnelly were also the same size but Dad and Mr. Donnelly were not the same size Mr. Donnelly was much taller. Her oldest son was in college and she gave mom lots of his clothes which fit Dad.

On our way home Mrs. Olivia yelled something to Mom as we went by but Mom couldn't hear her so Dad backed up the truck for them to talk.

Mrs. Olivia said, "My God what do you have in those big boxes?"

Mom said, "Stop by tomorrow and I will show you."

This was the lady who had worked for Mrs. Donnelly and refused the used clothes before they were given to Mom. Now she wanted to know what we had been given by the Donnelly's.

I asked Mom why tomorrow? Mom said, "My family comes first, don't you think so?"

I said, "Yes."

When we arrived home and finished dinner we opened the boxes which were the boxes Mr. Donnelly had given to us. These were new items that were from the store which Mrs. Donnelly had packed in the boxes.

Dad said, "Barbara, you and little Barbara hit the jackpot this time."

Mom said, "Little Barbara is my good luck charm." Everyone laughed and Mom divided all the clothes among us equally. Mom and Dad also had the same amount of clothes given to them.

I said to mom, "Isn't it strange that the Donnelly's gave us these things?"

Mom answered and said, "I think you are right Little Barbara."

The very next day Mrs. Olivia came down the road and Mom invited her in. They chatted a while and Mom told us to go and get the things the Donnelly's had given us. We went and got the things we had received.

Mrs. Olivia said to mom, "Those things look new. She never offered me any new things.

Mom said, "Some of these things are old and some are new." When someone asks if you can use some used clothes you have to take the used things and just maybe new ones will be in the mix as well." Many times they just want to see if you will take the used ones and if so then maybe new ones will be included."

When Mrs. Donnelly asked me could I use some used clothes I said, "Yes, I have a big family and I need all the clothes I can get."

Mom said, "If someone gives you something take it no matter what it is and one day they may give you things like the Donnelly's gave to me.

Mrs. Olivia dropped her head and said, "I messed up real bad."

The mom said, "Now you know better for the next time." You can always use things and remember you have a sick little girl you need all the help you can get sometimes."

Mrs. Olivia thanked mom and went home after their little talk and had quite a change of heart.

CHAPTER 14

Mr. and Mrs. Donnelly

In Mr. and Mrs. Donnelly's store were things my mom needed to make cakes, pies and other sweets. Mom didn't have much money so she ordered what she could afford. Mr. Donnelly was in the store that particular day and said to mom, "Mrs. Barbara I know you need more than what you've ordered.

Mom answered him saying, "Yes, I do, but I don't have the money."

He said to Mom, "I will make a deal with you, if you make me five sweet potato pies and one cake you can get all the ingredients you need to bake with.

Mom said, "Ok you've got a deal." He then wrote everything down and said he would deliver it the following day. She thanked him and we left.

Mom went right home and started baking. She made six sweet potato pies and two cakes. The other pies and cakes would be made for us when she received the rest of her baking ingredients. Mom only had a little flour left and had to wait until Mr. Donnelly delivered the items she'd ordered. With the little she had left and the flour she'd sent Tyler to buy, Mom baked some sweet potato pudding and peach pudding.

The next morning she was up early and had baked a table full of goodies. It was the week of camp meeting for the white people and this was the reason Mr. Donnelly wanted the pies and cakes. When he arrived at the house with the things Mom had ordered, he walked in the house and said to my mom, "Mrs. Barbara it sure smells good in here. Can I move in with you and your family? Everyone had a big laugh and mom told him O.K but when there's no smell of pies and cakes then you'll want to go home and besides Betty will not let you stay."

He said, "I guess you're right."

When he saw all the pies, cakes and other goodies on the table, he asked mom to sell him all of what she had baked at that time. Mom sold him everything and he took the baked goods and paid for all of it even the five sweet potatoes pies and the cake.

Mom said, "You're giving me too much money, with some of the goods you've already paid me."

Mr. Donnelly said, "Don't worry about it." Mom had Tyler help him put everything in the back seat of his car. He and Mom were so excited that they'd almost forgotten the things she'd bought from him earlier. He thanked my mom repeatedly, got in his car and started to turn around then remembered the items he had for Mom.

He said, "Barbara I almost forgot to give you the things I'd brought over." He asked Tyler to help him take the things in the house and as they brought them in, Mom had only expected a few things. What she found was much more than she expected. She received all the things she asked for and then some.

Mrs. Donnelly also had sent mom a recipe for pecan pies and a lot of things that she hadn't asked for as well.

Now the Donnelly's were white and had moved from up north which was one of the reasons we felt they were so nice. Many of the white's that had been born in the south didn't like the Donnelly's being so nice to blacks. They would give credit to the blacks when the others wouldn't and of course this caused quite a stir.

The Gordon family also had a store just around the corner; one of the sons decided to pull out from the family business and built a bigger brick store with a TV in it. Oh yes, some of their customers left the Gordon family store and start purchasing from the son because they would watch TV while shopping. The customers would purchase small items from the son's store with the TV but big purchases were made at the Donnelly's store.

Mr. Gordon was very nice but his wife, Mrs. Gordon, was a mean cuss. She would not sell Coca Cola to black people. When they wanted to buy Coca-Cola she said it was only for the white people and Pepsi was for blacks.

One day a black man named Mr. Greg and his son walked into the store and he purchased his son a Coca-Cola opened it and gave it to his son. Mrs. Gordon got mad as hell and took it out of his hands. All hell broke loose and Mr. Greg told her to give his son back the Coca Cola.

She said, "No go get a Pepsi."

Mr. Gordon came from the back of the store because he knew his wife. He told her your customers are always right.

Mrs. Gordon said, "Those monkeys are not right in my store they have to do what I say." Mr. Gordon slapped the hell out of her and dragged her to the back where they started fighting. He sent for his mother from the store across the street who took over while he took his wife home.

We didn't see Mrs. Gordon for quite a while. Finally one day she was back and after the incident which had happened she was much nicer. Everyone wanted to know what the hell he'd done to her for her to change so much that she was even nicer to the Donnelly's.

Mom was working for the Donnelly's one day and I was playing with their daughter Betty. We had lunch in the backyard while mom and Mrs. Donnelly went back to work. We asked if we could stay outside and play tag. While we were playing, a delivery truck came and the delivery man jumped out of his truck grabbed Betty and told me to, "Keep your black hands off of her." I started screaming and Mom and Mrs. Donnelly came running outside.

She said, "Let her go, "They can play together and touch each other too.' The delivery man, Mr. Rodger didn't like what she said.

He said to Mrs. Donnelly, "Where do you come from? Down here we don't mix with the black people because they might rub off onto us."

Mrs. Donnelly said to him, "Come into my office I need to have a little talk with you."

She said, "You children can go back and play."

We didn't want to play anymore after what had happened. She asked my mom if she'd like to come into her office while she talked to this young man.

Mom said, "No."

They stayed in the office for about fifteen minutes and when that young man came out he was a different person.

He said to Betty and me, "I'm sorry."

He said something to Mom, shook all of our hands saying again, "I'm sorry for acting like that."

It was as if he had been born again. The next time he came to deliver and my mom and I were there, he gave Betty and me a big kiss when he was leaving. I tried to wipe it off but of course it didn't work.

Mom asked Mrs. Donnelly what she had said to the young man.

Mrs. Donnelly said, "I put the fear of God in him."

I likened this to what Dad must have done to Red, the mule. He put fear in him and he started acting right or maybe it was the whipping Dad gave him. Sometimes I thought Red was going to kill Dad but he would calm down and listen to him.

Dad cleaned Red up and came to camp meeting to bring some wood. Red would be stepping like he owned the world. He was a beautiful cross mule horse.

Red was given his name because his color was red and everyone loved to see him when he came to camp meeting. Dad liked to drive Red more than his truck and everyone knew them as Red the mule and the one-horse wagon. No one else could handle Red except Dad and Nell would listen to Mom.

That year was the best camp meeting ever and Mom left thanking God.

CHAPTER 15

Mom and Dad's Big Secret

It was amazing to find out there was still something we didn't know about Dad. We thought we knew everything because he would tell us things all the time when he was drinking, but he never told us *this* secret he had. No one in the family ever told us about *this* secret.

Tyler was playing baseball with two brothers Bobby and Billy and others. Billy started cheating and an argument arose followed by a big fight.

Bobby said to Billy, "Stop fighting Tyler! You know his father killed a man.

Tyler said, "Take that back, my Dad didn't kill anybody. Take it back!"

My teacher, Mrs. Conway, knew all about this secret and came out of the school house to stop the fight. As usual, it was lunch time and we were sent home. She told us, "Go home and ask your Mom and Dad about it." We took off for home with Tyler walking as fast as he could. We could hardly keep up. I had to run to keep pace with him. Tyler put our little sister Golda on his back and the rest of us were on our own. I never knew we could get home as fast as we did that day.

When we arrived home we were all out of breath but not so much that we couldn't talk to Mom about Dad.

Tyler asked Mom, "Did Dad kill a man?"

Mom said, "I knew something was wrong and I knew this day was coming when I saw you all walking so fast in the middle of the day."

Mom said, "Put your books away and change your clothes and come to the barn house, I will tell you all what happened while we pick peanuts." We looked at each other and no one said a word.

I said, "Mom we don't want to wait that long please tell us now."

Mom said, "Well then, yes, he did."

My heart fell to my feet I couldn't move for a little while. All of us were in shock at that moment. We didn't know what to say what to do or think. Romeo and Golda started crying and as much as I liked to talk I was speechless and really mad. I was so mad I wanted to hit something, but I didn't know what to really do right then.

I realized I was mad at Dad until we all started listening to my mom. She told us what happened while we were supposed to be picking peanuts. Our hands were moving but our ears and eyes were glued on Mom's every word.

Mom said, "Mrs. Peggy was sweet on Dad or they were sweet on each other. She said, "She didn't know if they were lovers or not, but she always knew she was sending notes to him telling him to meet her at the Dew Drop Inn. When he didn't go she went and told her husband that Gil was messing with her trying to have sex with her.

Mom said, "Peggy had that going all over town."

Mom heard that her husband came to Dad asking if there was any truth to this rumor. Dad said, "No."

Grandpa told Dad, "If there was any truth to it, please stop before someone gets hurt." The rumors kept floating around then Peggy's husband, Mr. Paul, went back to Dad and asked if he was having an affair with his wife.

Dad again said, "No I wouldn't do that to you." The rumors continued even to the next little town.

Mr. Marty, a friend of Dad's, was having a party and Mrs. Peggy heard Dad was going to be there. She told her husband that your dad was still after her, trying to have sex with her and she needed him to beat Dad's ass for what he was trying to do with her.

Mrs. Peggy, her husband and son went to the party to beat Dad up. Mr. Paul and his son Peter, Mrs. Peggy had a baseball bat and sticks to whip or kill him. Someone said they were out there to beat Dad up and he went to the front door. There they were at the front door so Dad decided to go to the back door and they followed him there. Dad didn't want any trouble so his friend, Mr. Marty said, "Go to my bedroom and jump out the window." He did that and by the time he hit the ground the three of them were already there beating on him.

Dad tried to fight back whichever way he could but with three beating on him it was difficult. He had no leverage because they had the best of him at that moment in time. Dad begged and begged them to stop but they kept right on beating him. Dad felt like they were going to kill him so he put his hand in his pocket and pulled out his knife. He opened it with his teeth and stabbed the first person he could get to—which was Mr. Paul.

Even though Mr. Paul had been stabbed Mrs. Peggy and her son continued to beat on him. When they finally realized Mr. Paul had been stabbed the beating stopped. Dad got up and ran home. At that time, we only had a few children.

When he got home he told Mom what had happened.

He said, "They're trying to kill me."

Dad said, "I think I hurt Paul real bad but I don't know for sure."

The following day the police went to Grandpa Edgar's house and ask him to go with them to get your dad because Paul died. He went with them to our house, when they got there Grandpa got out and went in the house. He said to your father, "I guess you know why I'm with the police. Paul died."

Dad said, "I was hoping he was still alive and not dead."

Grandpa said, "Come peacefully."

Dad said, "Ok first I have to talk to Barbara."

He told Mom, "I don't know what's going to happen to me but try to hold it together." Then he walked out the door to the police car.

Now they jumped out the car to put handcuffs on him. Dad said, "No handcuffs."

The police went to put them on him anyway until Grandpa said, "He will be alright without them."

The police locked Dad up and thanked Grandpa for giving them a helping hand. They took Grandpa home and thanked Grandpa again. When Dad went in front of the judge he told Dad, "You're being held over for pre-trial." Dad was in jail for about three months then Mr. Whitehead got Dad a lawyer before the pre-trial.

People were talking about Dad going to jail for fifty years or life. Mrs. Peggy was putting some of those lies out as well. All kinds of different versions of the lies were being told. I wonder how Mrs. Peggy felt about her part in her husband's death.

It is now time for pre-trial and it turned out to be self defense and Dad was a free man. I now understood why people were afraid of Dad.

After mom finished telling us about our father, we were afraid of him for a little while. Mom told Dad he would have to talk to us because we were afraid of him. Dad got all of us together and sat down with us for a talk.

He said, "I'm sorry you children are afraid of me, I would never hurt one of you." What happened to Paul and me wasn't my fault. I never wanted anything to happen but I thought they were going to kill me. I did what I did to save my life. It was him or me."

Dad said, "I'm not a monster, I love all of you. Barbara and my children are all I live for. I truly love Barbara and my children, there is nothing I would not do for all of you."

Little by little we stopped being afraid because we knew in our hearts that Mom and Dad loved us and we loved them too. With Dad talking to us he won our love back and we found out that Paul was Dad's uncle. Yes, he was our uncle and everything was alright. Love heals all faults and things were now back in order.

CHAPTER 16

No More Farming

After the way Mr. Whitehead treated Mom about the bail and scraps of cotton and seeing the way things really went as well as the big liar Mr. Whitehead was she decided to let scrapping cotton go. For quite a while Mom tried to tell Dad how deceitful he was but of course Dad wouldn't listen. She explained that Mr. Whitehead never told the truth and still Dad, having a mind of his own, didn't believe her.

Due to the fact that Dad couldn't write his name or read he could only make an X or take an I.O.U, Mr. Whitehead got over on Dad quite a bit. Mom could never understand why we were always in debt when she would go to New York and work during the winter and Dad worked for DuPont and forever had debt hanging over their heads.

During the last year in Georgia while Mom was in Rochester, New York we talked Dad into getting us a record player. He was really high at that time. We never let him see it until Lucille ordered the records. She ordered B.B. King, Jimmy Reed, and Bobby Blue Bland with the money she got from her boyfriend.

Before Dad bought the record player he used to play the harmonica when he was drinking and did a great job which was almost as good as Jimmy Reed. We would go in the yard and dance our little asses off. I don't know who was the happiest, the children or our Dad. When he wasn't drinking he could hardly hit a note.

While Mom was in Rochester, Dad was running around with his women and we were at home having great fun.

The last year we spent in Georgia farming, Dad planted twenty-five acres of cotton. The years before, he would only plant fifteen acres because he was trying to get out of debt with Mr. Whitehead to please mom. She stayed in New York until it was time to pick cotton. Mr. Whitehead hired people to help Dad in the field when the cotton was ready to pick. Mom came home with Lucille and Mable to pick cotton. Tyler had to give up his job that year to help Mom and Dad get out of debt.

That was a very good cotton crop for Mom and Dad that year. Information was given to Mr. Whitehead about a man who was able to pick five hundred pounds of cotton a day. He hired this man to pick the cotton for him and Dad. He picked the cotton along with the bow and everything else he could find. In his picking he included the cotton sticks, leaves and the bush as well. Everyone else picked only the cotton.

Dad spoke to him about the way he was picking the cotton.

He told Dad, "I don't have time to pick all those things out."

Dad told him, "You better take the time because I am paying you to pick cotton nothing else.

Mr. Karl kept doing the same thing and Dad again told him "You are fired I can't use you anymore."

Mr. Karl said, "You can't fire me, you didn't hire me."

Dad said, "Get you things and get the hell away from here and me."

He left the field and went and found Mr. Whitehead who asked Dad what was the matter. Dad showed him Mr. Karl's cotton. He was surprised to see his cotton picked the way it was.

Mr. Whitehead asked Mr. Karl why he was picking cotton on his farm like that.

Mr. Karl said, "I pick cotton everywhere I go the same way. Then he said everyone else is very happy with my picking."

Dad said, "They were not happy with his work they were afraid of you Mr. Whitehead.

Mr. Karl asked Dad "Was he afraid of Mr. Whitehead."

Dad said, "No I am not afraid of him. If I was, I couldn't give him my best crops." Dad told Mr. Karl he was fired again and looked at Mr. Whitehead."

Mr. Whitehead then said, "You heard the man and walked away."

Dad weighed his cotton and took off half and paid him the rest. Mr. Karl was mad as hell with both of them. My family had worked hard to get out of debt; I even worked a little harder myself that year.

When Mabel, Lucille and Tyler came back home, I felt like all my family was back. They are the ones who grew up with me. I knew all of the others but they were not around me like Tyler, Lucille and Mable. I was extremely happy to see them.

After we finished picking cotton, Mabel and Lucille went back to New York. Tyler however didn't return. Mom and Dad went into Mr. Whitehead's office to see if they were out of debt and Mr. Whitehead confirmed they were out of debt. Dad and Mom asked are you sure Mr. Whitehead? He replied yes and they walked out of his office feeling very good.

Mr. Whitehead thanked them for the best crop of the years they'd planted. Mom walked out of his office and told Dad she wasn't going to farm anymore. She told him she was going to take her children and move up north. Dad said, "He wasn't ready to move from Georgia he was going to stay and continue farming for Mr. Whitehead.

Mom said, "Stay if you want."

Three days later Mr. Whitehead came and told Dad he had a few more I.O.U's. Dad said, "Why you didn't tell me when I was in your office?"

He said, "I found them after you left."

Dad said, "Let me see the I.O.U.!"

When he checked he told Mr. Whitehead, "These are not my I.O.U's nor is that my X. I know my X Mr. Whitehead."

Mr. Whitehead said, "Gil you was drunk when you made the X."

Dad said, "I don't give a damn how drunk I was, I know my X and how I make it.

Dad had to make an X because he couldn't read or write very well. This was the reason Mr. Whitehead was able to cheat Dad from year to year. He was so mad at Mr. Whitehead that he walked away to keep from hurting or killing him.

Dad changed his mind about moving up north and said to Mom, "That Motherfucker has been cheating me all these years and I am ready to go." Dad couldn't get over the fact that Mr. Whitehead was not trustworthy and how he had been keeping him farming telling lies about the I.O.U.'s

Dad said, "That son of a bitch! I will show him how to cheat. He said, "I got something for him just wait and see." Dad sold Mr. Whitehead's mules and did not have a problem doing so. Everyone loved Red, the mule, and in order to buy him the person buying had to buy Nell as well. Mr. Lucas came and bought both Nell and Red as soon as he heard about Dad selling the mules and actually paid more than was asked for the mules.

Dad sold all of Mr. Whitehead's farm equipment along with any and everything he thought was valuable enough to sell that belonged to Mr. Whitehead. He didn't move in the middle of the night like some of the other farmers, but decided to leave in the middle of the day.

Mom said, "What are we going to do if he comes around?"

Dad said, "That son of a bitch will not come by here and if he does I will gut him like a fish. He better not fuck with me and my family." I knew Dad meant every word he said.

Mable and Lucille went back to New York and we missed them. Mable was the funny one of the siblings. She was singing a song which said I am a man. I made twenty one and it was really funny when she was singing. Dad heard her singing and told Mom you better see about that gal she is hollering I am a man. Of course we all knew it was a song but Dad didn't know and we all started laughing when he told Mom she better see about that gal.

Mom finally told Dad that it was a song and we just had a little more fun laughing at Dad because he didn't know.

They have returned to Rochester, New York and we were missing them something terrible. Tyler however did not return to his job and stayed to help us move to Irvington, New Jersey. He took us to New Jersey in his '49 Ford. Seven of us travelled in that little car, and thank God we made it safely.

As we traveled along the way there was lots of snow which we had never seen before. Mom had seen snow when she traveled to New York and the closer we got to Irvington, New Jersey, the more snow we encountered. Because we had never seen snow before, we all became afraid with the exception of Mom who had seen snow.

Tyler assured us that there was nothing to be afraid of and that everything would be alright. Later as we traveled on we stopped to get something to drink and use the restroom. We had no idea where we were exactly but I knew things were different.

Being from the south there were a lot of things that we were not used to doing or seeing, of course using the bathroom with white people was one of those things.

CHAPTER 17

A New Beginning in Irvington, New Jersey

It was such a pleasure being in a different place and having a fresh start. I went into the bathroom looking for Mom, a white lady was also in there and I started to run because in Georgia, we weren't allowed to go to the same bathroom as the whites. She told me, "You can come on in we are not like the people in the South. Is that where you're from?"

I said, "Yes Ma'am."

Then mom walked out of the stall. I went looking for her because I knew we were not supposed to be in the same restrooms as the white people.

When we arrived in Irvington, New Jersey there was still snow on the ground. I was glad we didn't have to ride anymore. We moved in with our sister, Hilary, and her family. This was one of the sister's I really didn't like or get along with. If it had been up to me I wouldn't have moved in with her but it wasn't my decision I had to go along with what Mom and Dad chose to do.

I looked around at the town and to me, it was very strange because we were not used to big city life. Although I didn't want to be with Hilary and her family it turned out to be quite nice for all of us. Hilary still had her ways but I fell in love with her children

Living farming life we didn't have the chance to celebrate holidays like Halloween. We'd heard a little from Mom about it but didn't do any celebrating.

Hilary and her family began to tell us all about celebrating Halloween and this peaked our interest so we were looking forward to this celebration. They had explained about trick-or-treating and we were now ready to see what it was all about. After hearing so much about it, we were surprised to only be able to go on one street. We found out that this was because they didn't want us to get lost. We went such a long way that we became too tired to walk back but thank God we had some money on us because some of the people didn't have candy and gave us money instead. However before we decided to return, the people were laughing at our costumes because we were dressed as hoboes and they laughed and laughed at us until they couldn't laugh anymore.

We'd walked so far and knowing it was too far to walk back, our nephew said, "We can take the bus back home."

I asked him, Are you sure you know how to take the bus?"

He said, "Yes, I know how."

I was praying he knew how to get back to his house because we had so much candy, apples, oranges and more that we couldn't walk back home.

Mom and Hilary went through all of the goodies we'd received and made sure there was nothing to make us sick. They forgot one thing we'd already eaten so much candy before we ever came home. All of us became sick but the castor oil made us well. After everyone was better, Mom went out looking for work and found a job working for a doctor.

After Mom had worked for Mr. Turkey for a while, she and Mable decided to look for an apartment and found a store-front apartment. Mable and her son Skip moved in with us to help Mom out. I really didn't like the store-front apartment. I asked myself, what next can happen to me and found out that my new teacher here in town owned our apartment. Oh hell no! Besides my apartment problems, I started having other problems in school. With me being from the south I had a very bad accent. Every time I opened my mouth, my classmates would laugh their asses off. It got to the point I stopped talking and my teacher had to talk with Mom about my accent. They worked something out for me to stay after school one hour to read to Mrs. Taylor. This helped to keep the other children from laughing at me. I didn't like Irvington, New Jersey but I had to put up with it.

Everyday when I got out of school, I ran home and locked the door. I didn't want anyone to see me going into the store front apartment. I started looking for something to wear to school the next day. I didn't have many clothes to wear being in a new place.

It wasn't like the south where you could wear your clothes for a few days. If you wore the same clothes two days in Irvington, the children were mean and had a big laugh at your expense. They already had enough to talk and laugh about me. I tried to mix and match my clothes so they would look like I was wearing something different everyday.

Mom had a big box she kept our clothes in so we had to make due until she could do better. We didn't have much furniture that's why I didn't want anyone to know where we lived. My mother couldn't understand why I felt the way I did. She said, "I should be glad to have some place to live. Not realizing what I was going through I though about how much better the house we had in the south was for us.

Looking for something to wear the next few days of school I found a dress of mine that I'd worn before but it had a hole in it. I went looking for the needle and thread to sew my dress. I was able to fine both. Before I could sew my dress, my brother, Romeo, came home and started playing around me.

The first thing, I said to him, "I have a needle, don't play around with me."

He thought I was kidding when all of a sudden the needle went into his big thumb like all the way through to the other side. At first Romeo didn't feel anything and then it began to hurt. I felt so bad about it but I had warned him to stop playing around me.

I began crying and couldn't stop, Romeo was the one hurt with the needle in his thumb but he was trying to comfort me. By that time Mom and Mable came home. Mom asked Romeo what was wrong with me.

I said, "I it's not me, it's Romeo."

I told them what had happened and Mom started yelling at me. Romeo said, "It's not her fault. She told me she had a needle and I didn't believe her and I kept on playing around with her." Mom loved her boys dearly. I guess because she only had three boys and nine girls so she was very close to the boys.

Mom then asked me, "Why didn't you put the needle down."

I said, "I thought he was going to stop playing around when I told him I had the needle." Mom gave me a mean look and they took

Romeo to the hospital. When they returned, Romeo said there was a big fat nurse at the hospital who'd put him on her lap and held him so the doctor could give him a shot. She was still holding him when the doctor pulled the needle out of his thumb. The doctor told him the shot he had was for the pain and Mom was given medicine for him to take later for the pain.

After the incident with Romeo and the needle, I started getting sick. I kept telling Mom how I felt and was told that I was lazy. I began to have a headache every month real bad and the only one who'd believe me was my sister, Hope. She had a talk with me and asked me about my pain. I told her every first of the month my head would hurt so, so bad sometimes I could hardly lift my head.

One day Hope was home with me and could see for herself how much pain I was having. Hope believed me and spoke to Mom telling her that I wasn't lazy. She said, "Barbara would have told you all of the month not only the first of the month. Mom still didn't believe her or me. Hope asked mom to take me to the doctor to make sure but Mom was sure I was just lazy. Mom paid Hope no mind at all no not one bit.

One Sunday, Hope came by and everyone was outside playing. Hope asked Mom if I could go home with her for a week or two.

She said, "Yes."

Hope helped me get my things and put me in her car with her husband, Travis, her son, Travis Jr, and we went to her house. The following day Hope took me to the hospital. The doctor kept me in the hospital for a long time. They took every test they could think of to find the problem.

What was causing these headaches and why my period hadn't started was the question on everyone's mind. I was now about fourteen years of age then and after all the test they re-examined me and told Hope and me that my blood vessel was pressing on my nerve tissue and this was causing my headaches. My period was trying to go up instead of coming down.

The doctors started treating me in the hospital. I had a very nice black nurse who showed me how to crochet and knit and would sometimes have lunch with me. The treatment that they were giving me was to make my period go in the right direction instead of backing up. Trixie was the nurse's name which was really different because in the south black nurses were a no, no and you only saw white nurses. It seemed like the order of things was not right because I wasn't around a black nurse before. She was able to win me over and make a real difference in my life.

My first period was one of the worst pains I'd ever had causing me to stay in the hospital for such a long time. They knew I would be in a lot of pain. The doctor's wanted me there to watch me and help me through this difficult time. Once or twice they gave me something to ease the pain and knock me out for a while. Hope came to the hospital everyday and her husband and son would visit me on the weekends. Hope had a very nice husband and son.

My mother came once and that's when I began to think that Hope was more of a mother to me than my own mother. This made Hope and me very close more than any of my other sisters with the exception of Mabel.

Whenever my period came on, Mom would have to get a prescription every month for me. Mom said that the medicine cost too much and started getting over the counter medicine for me from the drugstore. The medicine helped a little but she still felt I was lazy because the severe pains began to come right back but not quite as bad as the first time.

All of my girls have gone through the same thing during their period, God bless the moms of all girls.

CHAPTER 18

Barbara and Tansy

The ordeal with the changing to the over-the-counter medicine has begun to work in my body and things returned to somewhat normal. Mom has decided to now move to Newark, New Jersey. I didn't like Newark either; it was no better than Irvington, New Jersey.

In Newark I did however like the school much better and had made a few new friends. Although I now have new friends one of them turned on me and that's why I really don't like women as friends. During those days girls were just girls and one of them I though was my friend I found out later really wasn't.

I was very smart in math and art and helped some of the girls in high school with their math. That's was how good I was in the subject of math.

Mrs. Winslow chose to have a contest with everyone in Art and of course all started talking about who they thought was the best. There were two people who they thought would be the best during the contest, that was my friend Tansy and me. This was when I really found out she wasn't my true friend. Tansy was a great artist in drawing and figured she would win the contest. I didn't think that I was going to win I just *hoped* I would win.

Time finally came for judging and everyone was on pins and needles. The teacher said, "The runner up is Tansy!" She turned blue because she always got her way with things. She was angry as hell when she went back to her seat. She looked at me with a real mean look. Mrs. Winslow then announced that I was the winner. I went to receive my prize and on my way back to my seat Tansy put her foot out and tripped me ripping my drawing. When I got up she kicked me and the fight was on. Mrs. Winslow and some of the bigger boys stopped us from fighting and we were taken to the principal's office.

She explained what had occurred and the principal said to Tansy, "You should be ashamed of yourself fighting with this little girl. You are much bigger than she is. I don't want to see you back in my office anymore."

He said to me, "The next time someone hits you in school, tell the teacher." He didn't say what I could do outside of the school house. Mr. Nelson sent Tansy home first and told her to go straight home. He then waited five minutes and sent me home. When I turned the corner there was Tansy. She grabbed me and the fight was on again. I was only five feet and she was five feet seven inches. She beat me unmercifully. I didn't have time to look around for leverage as Tyler had taught me earlier. The only thing I could do was reach up and scratch her. I knew I had long finger nails so I put them to use.

Tansy beat the cowboy shit out of me. When I arrived at the apartment, Romeo helped me up the stairs. I was so sore and could hardly walk. Romeo ran me a tub of water and he put some alcohol in the water. I took a bath and went to sleep. Romeo and I always cooked dinner together but today he was on his own. I couldn't move one inch.

The next day I felt a little better and after two days I went back to school. When I got there everyone was telling me how I messed up Tansy's face. I didn't know what they were talking about. I knew I scratched her but I didn't know where, she was slinging me all over the place. She didn't come back to school for two weeks.

In the mean time I was wondering why she wasn't in school. I went to the mailbox and there was a letter for mom from the courthouse. Mom opened the letter stating Tansy and her mom were taking Mom and me to court. When we arrived at court, Tansy and her mother were already there and we sat down. A little while passed as we were waiting in the courthouse which was full of people.

Everyone was coming and going and we were still sitting there, the bailiff kept looking around then:

The judge said, "Who is next?"

The bailiff said, "We are waiting for the McKay Family."

Mom said, "We are here. We've been here all morning."

The judge said, "Where is your daughter?

Mom said, "Next to me."

He asked me to stand up and I did.

Then he said, "You can sit back down."

He called Tansy to come to the stand. She walked up and the

The judge said, "Tell me what happened."

I couldn't see her face because it was all bandaged up, but I knew she was going to tell some lies.

Tansy told the Judge, "Barbara caught me outside where she and her friends beat her up. Barbara's friends held me down while she scratched my face. Then they all jumped me."

I didn't open my mouth

When she was finished it was now my turn and I told the judge that not one word from Tansy was the truth.

I said, "This started from a drawing contest which I won and she was mad. As I returned to my seat, she tripped me and I fell on the floor ripping my drawing as I got up. When I got up she then kicked me and we started fighting. Mrs. Winslow our teacher took us to the principal's office and he had a talk with us. He sent her home first and waited five minutes then sent me home.

The principal told Tansy to go straight home and when I turned the corner to go home, someone grabbed me and we started fighting. She was swinging me round and round everywhere and the only thing I could do to defend myself was to scratch her. I didn't mean to hurt her. I am so sorry for that!"

I can't say I wasn't afraid because I was so afraid I could hardly talk.

When I had finished the judge said, "I have two different stories, can either of you prove what you are saying?

I said, "I can prove everything I've said."

The judge said, "Tell me how you can prove to me that you are right."

I said, "My teacher, Mrs. Winslow, the principal and over half the school."

Then the judge said, "You can sit back down."

I could see the judge looked like he believed Tansy. He then said, "The one that is not telling the truth after I check out your stories, I will send that one to jail."

Tansy jumped up and said, "I am not telling the truth. Barbara is right it's all my fault." Everyone was surprised to see it was Tansy not being truthful.

The judge said, "Everything Barbara said is the truth?"

Tansy said, "Yes it is the truth."

The judge then said to Tansy's mother, "Mrs. Lemuel I can't rule for your daughter, she had three chances to stop but she chose not to take any of them. It's her fault her face is messed up. I rule for Barbara."

Then he said, "The court is dismissed."

Tansy's mother was upset and mad with her for lying. She couldn't understand how this little girl beat her ass. She was more upset that Tansy brought her into the courtroom and made her look like a fool.

Tansy said, "Mom, I'm so sorry. I didn't want you to know she beat me up by herself."

Her mother was mad as hell and I don't know who she was more angry wit—Tansy or me. She really had wanted this to be my fault not her daughter's.

Mrs. Lemuel didn't say one word to me or my Mom. She just walked out of the courtroom. Tansy remained home for another week. She then returned to school and when I saw her face, I started crying. She told me not to cry and said she'd be alright.

I said, "I'm so sorry." She replied the same. We hugged each other then she said, "All this is on me for being so hard headed. I was used to getting my way all the time because I'm my mother's only child.

Then she said, "Do you still like to cook?"

I replied, "Yes." From that moment on we were alright.

About five years later I saw her again and her face was still the same. I started to ask her why she didn't get it repaired and before I could finish my sentence she stopped me and said, "I'll keep my scar as a reminder of what happened to me to keep me from doing the same thing again. It will help me stay out of trouble."

CHAPTER 19

Antoinette and Barbara

My sister, Lucille, was getting married and everyone was helping Mom get things ready. We were cleaning, fixing up the house, cooking and making sure everything for the wedding would be nice and pretty.

Mom asked me to stay down stairs because we didn't have a phone and when she called me from the window I was to go to the bakery to check on the wedding cake. Wow, Mom had forgotten to order the cake on time so the baker had to work her in with other orders he had. He told Mom to keep checking because he didn't know when the cake would be ready. Mom finally told me to walk to the bakery to check on the cake. I walked six long blocks to and from the bakery and was very tired. I was happy when the baker said the wedding cake was ready.

After walking so long I returned downstairs and called Mom to let her know the cake was ready. Mom then told me to come up take your bath and get ready while she and Tyler went to get the wedding cake.

As I walked into the apartment to do what Mom told me to do, Antoinette said, "Where have you been all day."

I said, "Taking care of something for Mom." She didn't ask what so I guess she just assumed I wasn't doing anything.

She then said, "What are you going to do now?"

I said, "Take a bath as Mom told me to do."

She said, "No you're not! Run some water in the tub and give my girls, Sandra and Selene, a bath.

I said, "I am not going to give your girls a bath because that's not my job."

I went into the bathroom and slammed the door. Antoinette ran into the bathroom and locked the door. She slapped me and all hell broke loose. I went crazy on her, I was thinking about the slap she had given Sherry a few years back and now she finally took her chance to slap me.

I knew with everything in me she wasn't going to get away with slapping us then and now was my time.

We were fighting all over the bathroom and my other sisters were trying to break the door open with no luck. Dad was sitting in the kitchen which was next to the bathroom but didn't move or say one word. We fought until Mom and Tyler returned from the bakery. Tyler opened the bathroom door but before he came in, I was trying to flush her head down the toilet. It was to no avail! I was too small and not strong enough, however I gave her a run for her money. I paid her back for the slap she gave Sherry and me. She thought she could beat me by locking the bathroom door but I put a hurting on her.

Following the fight I was very sore and Antoinette was waiting for Mom to beat me.

Mom said, "If you couldn't beat her why do you think I am going to do it?"

Mom said, "I've told you over and over again to keep your hands off your brothers and sisters; those are my children *not* yours. Barbara is *my* daughter, I tell her what to do not you."

Antoinette said, "Everyone was helping except Barbara."

Mom said, "That is where you are wrong. I had her doing something for me all day. She was walking back and forth to the bakery and you had the nerve to jump on her!" You got just what you deserved. The others let you beat them but not Barbara she can hold her own."

Mom said, "You will think twice before you hit her again."

From that day on, Antoinette and I were good together. She never hit Sherry or me again. I really felt sorry for what I did to my sister but I had to let her know I could fight too. It is funny that I am always sorry after a fight. I don't start the fights I just finish them most of the time.

The wedding turned out wonderfully well and Lucille was a beautiful bride. So many friends and family came over and some of them stayed over night to enjoy the festivities. Many of the family members were from out of town and we camped out on the floor like Indians.

When Lucille got married, I was only fifteen but even then, I knew that family was a force to be reckoned with. There had been some seriously crazy moments in my life, but without a doubt, I knew that someone in my family would always be there for me no matter what.

About the Author:

When I was twenty five I thought about writing a book but my spelling wasn't that good. I started and stopped and then gave up. I knew what I wanted to write about but I can't put it into words.

I tried but couldn't put it out of my mind. Now I have four grown children and my baby wrote a book. I told her, "I wish I could write a book."

She said, "Mom, if you put your mind to it, you will be able to write your book."

She gave me a dictionary that helped a little. It took too much time to look up all the words. Then I realized I had a dictionary in my children. That's when I started asking them to spell for me. I started with my son and grandson. If they were not around, I called my daughter in Tampa or Atlanta, Georgia or my daughter in Sanford.

The one who put the writing bug in me, was my little granddaughter and all of my grandchildren.

Thanks to my daughter.

This book is about growing up on a farm and knowing my father wasn't perfect. It's about how my mom helped people and it's also about children helping and working hard. You'll read about Dad's women and about my sisters and brothers. This book is about Red the horse, Nell the mule, the birth of Barbara and a little blue dress. It's about a slap and picking cotton. It's about Mom taking food to old people whenever she could and I was right there with her. It's about lots of other things, too!